40

THRIVE

A Devotional Study for the Church, the Body of Christ

**To the Lord Who is all in all
(1 Corinthians 15:28).**

Be my all today and forever.

To my wife and children

*Words cannot tell your worth to me,
but I pray my life will convey to you undeniably
the fact the I love you more and more each day*

————————————————

**Unless otherwise indicated all scripture references are from
the King James Version.**

INTRODUCTION

As A.W. Tozer once said, "I want salty, down to earth realism." So, I am going to be blunt. In the 15 years of preaching, from eastern North Carolina all the way west to Texas, I have found one big problem within the American church. If you are a minister, I am fairly certain you would agree that it is the fact that churches have lost spiritual discernment. We are lacking in "making disciples." We might be a nation increased with physical obesity, but we are so anemic when it comes to godly understanding.

If statistics are correct, only about 5% of professed believers witness to others. Only about 15% read their bible on a regular basis. Paul revealed in Ephesians 4 what should be the aim of the church, *"Till we all come in the unity of the faith, and of the knowledge of the Son of God, unto a perfect man, unto the measure of the stature of the fulness of Christ: That we henceforth be no more children, tossed to and fro, and carried about with every wind of doctrine, by the sleight of men, and cunning craftiness, whereby they lie in wait to deceive; But speaking the truth in love, may grow up into him in all things, which is the head, even Christ* (Vs. 13-15)." Simply, it is that Christ be formed in every individual believer.

Burdened for people's lack of understanding over the truths of scripture, for years, I wrote (And still do) weekly articles for the Sunday morning congregation and for the city's newspaper. I never believed it to be much, but there were many times I had people from many different congregations and denominations tell me how much the articles helped them understand more of God's Word.

Not long ago, I felt led to gather different articles I had written to make a short booklet that would aid those in the church in personal study and growth. It is compiled of forty different articles with scripture readings for morning, noon, and night. Also, there are questions given to encourage the believer to dig deeper into many of the texts. Anyone can read this book, but it is designed as well for the pastor and his congregation to read it together for forty days. Forty days is a significant number in the scriptures. During the time of Noah, it rained upon the earth forty days and nights. Forty years the children wandered the wilderness. Moses was on Mt. Sinai for forty days. Jesus fasted in the wilderness for forty days. There are many other biblical examples, but for now I simply ask you, are you up for this devotional challenge?

Finally, I am nobody. There is nothing good in me except Jesus Christ. If these short studies help turn Christians back to the word of God and ultimately enlighten them to the call of daily surrender to the Holy Spirit, then I am pleased.

Simply a servant,

Joshua Horton

Day 1

Many people know what POW and MIA represent. They are military terms, which the first one means Prisoner of War, and the second, Missing in Action. It is a sad day for friends and families to hear that their loved ones are missing or taken captive, during battle. Sadly, even in the Christian life, there are "prisoners of war" and those "missing in action." I'm sure you can think of some. They once fought hard for Christ, but have abandoned the fight. They ran the race, only to make the bench their goal line. Because of steady bitterness, continuously giving into temptations, or constant frustration, they give up and go missing.

There are others who have allowed themselves to become "prisoners" in the war. Instead of being *transformed* in their minds into Christ-likeness, they have *conformed* themselves to the worldly fashion of today. They have brought themselves back in bondage, back to a foolish, sinful lifestyle. It is tragic, but to only focus on the negative actions of others, will not uplift the truth of Christ! The fact is that Jesus has given us victory! Sure we stumble. Sure we fall. In our power, we cannot face the battles that bombard our lives everyday. Without Jesus, we are nothing and can do nothing. All Christians must remember that they don't have to be a prisoner, for the war has been won through Jesus!

He is our victory! We don't have to end our battles in bitterness, but in blessings. Paul said in Colossians 1:29, *"Whereunto I also labour, striving according to his working, which worketh in me mightily."* It is not in us to fight alone and wage war. Christ has already won! He not only has the power to save us, but also the power to strengthen us everyday to walk the Christian life. If only Christians could grasp the truth of *"Christ in you, the hope of glory* (Colossians 1:27)," there would not be casualties on the field. Many Christians have become so accustomed to hearing messages about how they were saved to serve God and show Him how much they love Him by working as hard as they can for Him.

It is true that the purpose of salvation in Christ is not for someone just to get a free ticket ride to heaven, but for them to glorify God with their lives; however, what no one should ever forget is through the Holy Spirit, Jesus lives in the hearts of every believer. Man, woman, boy, girl. His Spirit is actively working in every Christian's heart, so give up the notion that God is sitting up in heaven beating you over the head, shouting "You better live FOR me!" No, God is gently and lovingly saying to us, "I am working THROUGH you. Be available to me, for I will give you the strength to serve." Do you believe He is working in your life? Are you available to His Will?

FOR TODAY
Read

Colossians 1 (Morning)
What are children of God strengthened by (vs. 11)?

2 Timothy 2:1-9 (Noon)
What is the aim of the believer in being a "good soldier" (vs. 4)?

Philippians 2 (Night)
As believers, how would "letting the mind of Christ be in us" affect our day to day behavior and walk (vs. 1-9)?

Where faith resides fear must retreat!

Day 2

Ephesians 6 is known as the "Armor of God" chapter. Over and over ministers have fervently preached on this particular chapter, listing each piece of armor and describing in detail what they mean to the believer. However, if one just focuses on the armor and not the rest of the passage, they will miss an essential element to being a "good soldier" of Christ. It is found in Ephesians 6:18, in which Paul exhorts believers that they are to be, *"Praying always with all prayer and supplication in the Spirit, and watching thereunto with all perseverance and supplication for all saints."* It is the call of deep, devoted prayer. To be more specific, it is the call of personal supplication and passionate intercession.

Richard Baxter once stated, "Prayer is the breath of the new creature." No Christian can truly be effective without having a prayer life. Heartfelt prayer is what gives us the courage to engage in the battle! It is in the hour of supplication where we can come to the place to, *"...be strong in the Lord, and in the power of his might* (Ephesians 6:10)." If we only focus on the armor and not the attitude of prayer, then we are like a child trying to wear heavy chain mail, while carrying a large metal shield. We will be too weak to stand firm and properly use the armor.

In verse 18, Paul exhorts believers to pray *"in the Spirit."* Literally, we are to come with a yielded heart, petitioning according to God's will. The Gill Commentary describes powerful praying as, "...with the heart, soul, and spirit engaged in it; it is put up with a true heart, and a right spirit, and without hypocrisy; in a spiritual way, and with fervency, and under the influence, and by the assistance of the Spirit of God." Also, in this passage, the word *pray* correlates with worship and the word *supplication* with requests. As soldiers of Christ, we come with hearts of worship, making requests to Him.

Finally, in the later part of verse 18, Paul states that believers are to watch *"thereunto with all perseverance and supplication for all saints."* We are called to intercede and pray for one another. No one should ever be a "lone ranger" in God's army. We are in this warfare fighting together, not against one another. We need to be reminded that our enemy is Satan and that a "good solider" not only wears every piece of armor, but also prays to the Lord seeking to encourage and edify fellow believers.

FOR TODAY
Read

Ephesians 6 (Morning)
What is the foundation in putting on the armor of God (vs. 10)?

2 Corinthians 2:1-11 (Noon)
According to this passage, what is one foothold Satan strives to get within the church body?

2 Samuel 22 (Night)
List all the depictions of God in this passage. Here's an example: "...he is a buckler to all them that trust in him (vs. 31)."

****Invariably taking up the armor of God stated in Ephesians 6 is not by daunting practices or daily principles, but it is in the Divine Person of Jesus Christ. We must put on Christ, for He is made unto us our, "...wisdom, and righteousness, and sanctification, and redemption." (1 Corinthians 1:30) Every facet of the Christian life is found in Jesus Christ alone***

8

Day 3

Just a few years ago, studies revealed that less than 40% of people who claim a religious background go to church services. Around 28% claim to attend at least once a week, 8% once a month, and 4% once a year. For many churches, there is a steady decline in membership each year. I have often been asked why so many people, especially young adults, leave the church and what can be done to ensure stability. Of course, the solution is not so easily attained. There are many reasons people hardly darken church doors.

It is all rooted in one's perception of the church, ranging from misguided notions that faith equals ignorance to hurt emotions one faced during a time of church conflict. Try to describe your view of the American church in one word. I will list some that I have heard others use: hypocrites, cultish, uninformed, divided etcetera. Now, you will find that many of the people that say such things are only mouthing what they have seen, heard, and read from liberal media, decadent entertainment, and cynical books. In fact, in my experience many of the so called "free-thinkers" (people who claim they started thinking for themselves and don't believe in God) understand very little of true science and what the bible really teaches.

However, as a whole in America, Christians have forgotten that they are called not just to "go to" church, but to be the Church. Jesus said in Matthew 28:19-20, *"Go ye therefore, and teach all nations, baptizing them in the name of the Father, and of the Son, and of the Holy Ghost: Teaching them to observe all things whatsoever I have commanded you: and, lo, I am with you alway, even unto the end of the world. Amen."* The greatest characteristic for a thriving church is discipleship. This is why so many people have left and why those who remain are at odds with one another. Church life is not about sitting in a pew, but about serving people. Discipleship stretches far beyond a class curriculum; it is about one surrendered soul edifying, admonishing, and encouraging another soul through God's truth. It is stated in Hebrews that we are not to forsake "...*the assembling of ourselves together*," but this same passage also calls us to exhort "...*one another: and so much the more, as ye see the day approaching* (10:25)."

Finally, what can be done for those who have been "turned off" to the church? Simply, point them to Jesus. Paul stated in Colossians 1:18, *"And (Christ) is the head of the body, the church: who is the beginning, the firstborn from the dead; that in all things He might have the preeminence."* Jesus is the Head of the Church. Don't try to "win" them to a congregation, but witness to them about Christ, our Savior!

FOR TODAY
Read

Hebrews 10 (Morning)
What do verses 10-14 reveal about the sacrifice of Christ and our sanctification?

Psalms 122 (Noon)
What made David so joyful?

Isaiah 38 (Night)
Because of the salvation of God, what did Hezekiah say he would do (vs. 20)?

Christianity today looks more like a mass industry of commercialism instead of the marvelous entity of Christ

Psalms 23 is a highly favored passage of scripture. It is almost always recited at funerals and often memorized by youth for church competitions. Sadly, for some people, this is the only chapter in the Bible that they know! I have met a number of people that are not even Christian, yet still have a deep appreciation for its beautiful style and comforting words. I truly believe one of the biggest reasons why Psalms 23 is so loved by many is because it is a great reminder of the amazing promises given when one follows the Great Shepherd, Jesus Christ.

When I read Psalms 23, I am reminded of the Christian journey. It begins with us confessing and acknowledging that *"The Lord is (our) Shepherd* (Vs.1)." It is then that we experience rest from the bondage of sin, restoration for our souls, and we are placed on the *"paths of righteousness for His name's sake* (Vs.2-3)." Along the way, the believer not only experiences mountain tops of success, but also dark valleys of suffering; however, it is in these times that God's faithfulness is manifested and His presence is all the more real (Vs.4). In verse 6, there is a future promise that the Christian will one day, "dwell in the house of the Lord forever."

What I would like to focus on though is verse 5, which states, *"Thou preparest a table before me in the presence of mine enemies: thou anointest my head with oil; my cup runneth over."* What does such "preparation" mean for the believer? It is a description of the banquet of blessings and grace that God gives everyday. Few believers come to realize the true abundance they have in Christ! In describing the oil, the Amplified Version states, *"It is difficult for those living in a temperate climate to appreciate, but it was customary in hot climates to anoint the body with oil to protect it from excessive perspiration. When mixed with perfume, the oil imparted a delightfully refreshing and invigorating sensation. Athletes anointed their bodies as a matter of course before running a race. As the body, therefore, anointed with oil was refreshed, invigorated, and better fitted for action, so the Lord would anoint His "sheep" with the Holy Spirit, Whom oil symbolizes, to fit them to engage more freely in His service and run in what he directs- in heavenly fellowship with Him."*

The devil wants us to look at the Christian life like we are starving, alone, and simply fighting in our own power to "make due" and somehow please the Lord. This is not the case! Ask God to open the eyes of your heart that you might fully realize the glorious victory and continual provisions that He gives through the indwelling of His Spirit! Do you truly believe that there is already a lavish table of grace and joy spread before you here and now, through the Spirit's power?

FOR TODAY
Read

Psalms 23 (Morning)
Ultimately, why does the Lord "lead us in the paths of righteousness (vs. 3)?"

John 10:1-18 (Noon)
What are the three intentions of the thief? The thief can be compared to whom (vs. 10)?

Ezekiel 34 (Night)
What was Ezekiel's cry against the shepherds (vs. 2-3)?

Life is most MEANINGFUL, when it is most WORSHIPFUL

Day 5

1 Corinthians 9:18-19 What then is my reward? That in my preaching I may present the gospel free of charge, so as not to make full use of my right in the gospel. For though I am free from all, I have made myself a servant to all, that I might win more of them

When I was a teenager, the church youth group of which I was part of filled out these weekly forms called "Teen Analysis." It was a point system such as each day that you read your bible you got 10 points, bringing a visitor to service that week got you 100 points and so on. Normally, the three teens with the highest amount of points in one year were able to go for free on a big, expensive, and upcoming youth trip. I look back now and find myself wondering why this was ever promoted. Did I ever win? Sure. Did I ever do it for the right motive? Hardly. Money and self-righteous bragging rights was the big factor.

In a regular business environment, one may often hear from certain management, "I don't care how you do it, just as long as it gets done!" This is not nor ever will be the case in Christianity. Motive is intertwined in ministry. Just "getting the job done" is not our call. You see, in the verses above, Paul revealed not only his mission, but also his motive in life. It may be a little hard to swallow but Paul's mission was to be a servant to all that he might more freely share the gospel. He could have easily stood himself up on some pedestal of religious pride, but instead he demoted himself so that God's Word would be promoted in the hearts of individuals. Perhaps the reason some of us don't witness is because we dare not step down off our soap box of piety. Our calling is simple: Serve that you can Share.

In verse 18, Paul declares that his reward and motive in serving is to ultimately glorify Christ in never hindering the testimony and truth of the gospel by the way he lives. If it meant his convenience over the gospels furtherance, he would choose to suffer every time, so that God's saving grace would shine forth to others all the more. Forget fame and fortune, forget pomp and pride, his mission was to further the gospel and his motive was to exalt the Savior. What about you?

FOR TODAY
Read

Philippians 1 (Morning)
Regarding the gospel, why was Paul joyfully encouraged (vs. 12)? What was Paul's primary aim (vs. 20)?

1 Corinthians 9:11-27 (Noon)
What ultimately was Paul's reward in preaching the gospel (vs. 18)?

Psalms 115 (Night)
What is the significance of what the Psalmist wrote in verses 9-11?
Hint: God's provision and protection was extended to whom?

Colossians 3:17 says, "And whatsoever ye do in word or deed, do all in the name of the Lord Jesus, giving thanks to God and the Father by him." In the Christian life, To "Do" for the Lord is simply Human activity, but To "Do" for and "Delight" in the Lord is Holy Activity

Day 6

For a few moments I would like to turn your attention to Psalms 33:1-5. To help you fully grasp the teaching in this passage, I am going to write a few notes between several verses.

1 Rejoice in the LORD, O ye righteous: for praise is comely for the upright.

At the very outset of the chapter, there is a call to rejoice in God. Yet, this call is given to those who are "righteous" or those who are trusting in and following after the Lord. True praise comes from God's children. In these verses, David gives many reasons why we should praise God. First, *praise is comely (suitable, beautiful) for the upright.* A life that is filled with praise to God reveals a heart that is close to Him. How long has it been since you genuinely praised God?

2 Praise the LORD with harp: sing unto him with the psaltery and an instrument of ten strings. 3 Sing unto him a new song; play skillfully with a loud noise.

Praising God is also attributed with music. God honoring songs seem to thrust our hearts even more into an attitude of adoration and thankfulness. We are called to honor God through our mouths and our music. If you can't play an instrument, then sing a spiritual song and if you can't sing, then hum a heartfelt hymn. Simply praise God!

4 For the word of the LORD is right; and all his works are done in truth.

Verse four reveals the second and third reasons we should praise God. Because we can rejoice in His perfect Word and because we can remember His wonderful Works! We have a sure foundation in the Word of God. It is trustworthy and powerful. Also, regarding the works of the Lord, we have a glorious promise stated in Romans 8:28, *"And we know that all things work together for good to them that love God, to them who are the called according to his purpose."* How much do

15

you dwell on the Word of God? How much do you trust the works of God?

5 He loveth righteousness and judgment: the earth is full of the goodness of the LORD.

The final reason we should rejoice in the Lord is because of His everlasting love and goodness made known throughout the earth. He is our provider, protector, and redeemer in this world. If we would simply take time to look at all the beauty God has made for us to enjoy and all the love He has given for us to experience, we would continually echo to our generation the call to REJOICE IN THE LORD!

FOR TODAY
Read

Psalms 33 (Morning)
The previous devotion only focuses on the first five verses of this passage; therefore, read the entire chapter and write down other reasons stated as to why we can praise God.

Hebrews 13:8-25 (Noon)
What is important about verses twenty and twenty one and why should it bring comfort to a believer's heart?

Revelation 19 (Night)
In this passage, what terms are ascribed to Jesus?

Christ's first coming was as a Lamb of Meekness, but His second coming will be as a Lion of Might

Day 7

John 3:16 is one of the most memorized verses in the Bible. It states, *"For God so loved the world, that he gave his only begotten Son, that whosoever believeth in him should not perish, but have everlasting life."* The gospel message is simplified and almost condensed into this one passage. Praise the Lord that the good news of God's love is to "whosoever believes!" What a glorious promise!

Yet, even though this particular passage is well known among Christians, many do not know 1 John 3:16, which reads, *"Hereby perceive we the love of God, because He laid down His life for us: and we ought to lay down our lives for the brethren."* John 3:16 deals with God's love manifested to the world, but the later reveals the call of believers to manifest God's love to one another.

As the longest living apostle, John witnessed (And I'm sure he experienced as well) many of the sufferings and hardships that the New Testament Church went through. He also saw the divisions and carelessness that would arise within certain church bodies. In the midst of such turmoil, he wrote of the love of God and how every Christian is called to exercise a deep, pure love; foremost to God, and then to fellow believers. We need to be reminded of this today. Jesus said, *"By this shall all men know that ye are my disciples, if ye have love one to another (John 13:35)."* This is the true mark of a Christian! Spiritual words on bumper sticker or a T-Shirt will never set us apart. Our faithfulness to God is manifested by how we love our fellow man. We show our true colors by loving!

Notice what Paul writes to the church at Ephesus, *"I also pray that love may be the ground into which you sink your roots and on which you have your foundation. This way, with*

17

all of God's people you will be able to understand how wide, long, high, and deep his love is. You will know Christ's love, which goes far beyond any knowledge. I am praying this so that you may be completely filled with God (Ephesians 3:17-19 / God's Word Translation)." If the love of God has penetrated and filled your heart, then it will surely flow into your actions.

This reckless, selfless, and committed love can never be counterfeited. I may be willing to spend a few bucks on someone else, but what about spending my own life? Ultimately, we need to get back to the presence of Christ, each day drawing closer to Him. As we "plant" ourselves in His presence, His love will grow in us and overflow to those around us.

FOR TODAY
Read

John 13 (Morning)
What was the significance of feet washing?

1 Corinthians 13 (Noon)
What does love "rejoice" in (vs. 6)?

1 Peter 1 (Night)
We are to love one another with what (vs. 22)?

Christian, the salvation of souls is your lifelong assignment, the power of the Spirit is your timeless aid, and the glory of God is to be your supreme aim

Day 8

Paul wrote in 1 Timothy 6:6-8, *"But godliness with contentment is great gain. For we brought nothing into this world, and it is certain we can carry nothing out. And having food and raiment let us be therewith content."* As a kid, I had a romanticized view of what adulthood was like. I often thought, "Boy, when I grow up, then I will be free to do anything and be able to buy whatever I want!"

Of course this is so far from reality, and now at times I catch myself day dreaming of my childhood to briefly escape the pressures of this life. Sadly, it is in our nature to believe that the "grass is greener on the other side." You only have to take one glance at the Israelites to realize this. From the moment their feet crossed out of the Red Sea, doubt and discontentment settled into their hearts. Their song of praise for God's deliverance soon turned into a skeptical composition of ingratitude.

This generation is marked by covetousness. Many have been deceived into thinking that if they just "get more," than they will be happy and live a freeing life. However, it is in contentment that we find genuine and enduring satisfaction. The reality is that joy and liberty blossoms, when one's contentment is rooted in Christ.

No matter what pressures this life may bring, we can rejoice in knowing that *"The Lord is (our) helper!"* Do you want to know what real freedom is? It's coming to the place where you daily rest in God's grace and trust His plans. It's letting go of seeking "the next big thing" and just marveling over the wonder and ways of God.

FOR TODAY
Read

1 Timothy 6 (Morning)
As Paul stated, what was the end result for many who "sought after riches?"

Proverbs 30:1-14 (Noon)
What was Agur's request to the Lord in verses 7-9? What does it reveal concerning contentment?

Revelation 3 (Night)
What was truly wrong with the Laodician church (vs. 17)? How can this be applied to Christians today?

ALL WE DESIRE

Nothing more, nothing less.

No materials we need possess.

Of these we are most content

Only fruit from His Spirit

and the nearness of His presence.***

Day 9

I have found it very uplifting and encouraging studying the prayers of different people in the Bible. Some are uttered in desperation, some cry out because of their sin, and others rejoice in prayer over God's goodness. One such prayer that is always dear to me is Jabez's prayer, which is stated in 1 Chronicles 4:10, *"And Jabez called on the God of Israel, saying, Oh that thou wouldest bless me indeed, and enlarge my coast, and that thine hand might be with me, and that thou wouldest keep me from evil, that it may not grieve me! And God granted him that which he requested."*

What is interesting is that even from his birth it did not appear that Jabez would grow up to experience many blessings, seeing that his name meant sorrow and grief. His mother named him this because of her own saddened state at his birth.

However, Jabez grew up fully knowing that a name does not dictate the blessings of life, but only by following the God of hope and love. It is said in verse 9 that he was more honorable than his brothers. I truly believe it was because he was a man of prayer and fully trusted God.

You may wonder, what was so important about his prayer? Let's look again at what he petitioned to God. First, he prayed for God's blessings (*bless me indeed*). Second, he sought for prosperity and spiritual growth (*enlarge my coasts*). Third, he prayed for God's presence (*that thine hand might be with me*). And finally, he requested for God to preserve and purify him (*keep me from evil*).

Oftentimes, when people pray, they only pray for blessings. They do not think to seek God's presence and rarely do they pray about living a pure life. I know, at times, this is the case with me. However, Jabez knew that true prosperity could only come by drawing close to the presence of God. May God teach us all that blessings and power flow greater through a pure life that longs to know Him more.

FOR TODAY
Read

1 Samuel 1 (Morning)
How did Hannah describe her prayer to the Lord (vs. 15)?

James 5:13-20 (Noon)
In verse 17, what is the believer reminded of concerning the powerful prophet Elijah?

Psalms 17 (Night)
What was the satisfaction and anticipation of David's heart?

*** *If there was nothing enjoyable handed down to us in this world, no gifts received, and no sunny days, we still have cause to be cheerful, for the kind interest that the Almighty has in us* ***

Day 10

You are not always promised a great harvest in gardening. It is true that I have sometimes met people who thought their crops were going to yield very little, only to find a much bigger harvest than the year before. However, for many farmers, due to dry weather, they have a disappointing return. Still, there is something that we can reap in our lives every time we plant the special seeds in humbleness. It is the harvest of joy. Nehemiah faithfully declared to the Isrealites, "*...the joy of the LORD is your strength*," yet it is missing in many homes and in many hearts today. We must realize that by the actions of our lives and the attitudes of our hearts we can plant seeds that will blossom into blessings and joy.

Paul stated in Acts 20:35, "*I have shewed you all things, how that so labouring ye ought to support the weak, and to remember the words of the Lord Jesus, how he said, It is more blessed to give than to receive.*" First, we must realize that a generous heart seeking to bestow kindness to others will ultimately reap in joy. Do not get caught up in the thought that you might receive something in return, but take heart in that every time you show genuineness and compassion, the light of the love of Jesus and the Gospel shines brighter.

Jeremiah 15:16 states, "*Thy words were found, and I did eat them; and thy word was unto me the joy and rejoicing of mine heart: for I am called by thy name, O LORD God of hosts.*" Secondly, a meditating mind on God's Word will produce joy. Do you daily read it? His Word is sustenance for our hearts and wisdom for our minds. Are you spiritually starving from not studying the Scriptures?

Finally, a trusting life yields the fruit of joy. Seeking to comfort many on a battered ship, Paul said in Acts 27:25,

"Wherefore, sirs, be of good cheer: for I believe God, that it shall be even as it was told me." God told Paul that no lives would be lost from their voyage. After the promise from God, Paul welled up inside with joy and was able to encourage many down trodden hearts. Why? He simply believed God. Do you believe God, do you trust Him? Would your finances reveal the answer? Would your attitude through problems speak volumes of bitterness and anger or of trust and hope?

FOR TODAY
Read

1 Timothy 6:5-15 & Acts 5:1-12
What was the attitude and sin of Ananias and Sapphira?

Psalms 119:1-16 (Noon)
Highlight the "I will" statements in these verses. Try to take one each day for a week, meditate on it and then say it out loud.

Isaiah 26 (Night)
According to Isaiah, how is "perfect peace" obtained?

What is God's perfect will? Amidst the masses clamoring it's "to be peaceful with everyone" and the pomp noise of religious leaders declaring that it's "to do as much as you can to serve Him," there is a faint whisper from the Holy Spirit to the humble heart gently saying, "It's Jesus. He is your life, so let go and let ME flow through your life."

Day 11

I remember reading an online news article about those who died in a church shooting at Charleston, SC and in the comment section someone wrote, "Where was God in all of this? If He is real, He would have stopped this!" This is the type of argumentation I have heard for many years. An evil man kills an innocent man, thus people blame the God they claimed not to believe in.

The Bible teaches that mankind has a free will and also that we live in a world of corruption (Romans 8:19-23). Jesus never hid this fact nor did He ever say that life would be easy. In fact, in Matthew 6:24 He states, "*So don't ever worry about tomorrow. After all, tomorrow will worry about itself. Each day has enough trouble of its own (GWT).*" Again, He said, "*These things I have spoken unto you, that in me ye might have peace. In the world ye shall have tribulation: but be of good cheer; I have overcome the world (John 16:33).*"

I had someone challenge me over why God would not stop wicked deeds. I began to explain how I sadly didn't believe most people would want God to stop ALL WRONG. Think about it. What if the moment a person seeks to commit adultery, they end up crippled for a week? What if when a person grabs a beer, with the intent of getting drunk, the beer bottle bursts in their hands? What if when someone is about to gossip, curse, or slander their mouth is forcefully shut for the whole day? No, I believe people would be angrier with God, if they couldn't act upon their evil intents, than they are when an atrocious act is committed.

You see, God has given every man a divine conscience and has placed His law within our hearts. He did not design us to be robots, for in this we could not choose to love Him. But we will definitely be held responsible for what we do. It amazes me in this country how a man can murder several people, and if by chance he does receive the death penalty, it would take many years before our judicial system ever carries out the sentence. Of course, when it comes to God, we want Him to act upon things immediately, and if He doesn't, somehow He has disproved Himself to us. We must realize that God knows all and will one day right all the wrongs of life. He has promised He will wipe away every tear from our eyes. He is the only Hope for this sin sick world. Let us never forget the exhortation to, "*Be not overcome of evil, but overcome evil with good* (Romans 12:21)."

FOR TODAY
Read

John 14 (Morning)
Highlight in this passage the comforting promises that Jesus gave to all those who trust in Him.

Hebrews 12:1-11
Why are we at times "chastened" of the Lord?

Revelation 7 (Night)
What nation and number of people did John see praising God (vs. 9)?

A Sincere Supplication

Keep my heart broken for a lost World
My mind sharp for the study of your Word
My body active for your Work
My entire life yielded to your Will*

Day 12

Colossians 3:22-23 states, *"Servants, obey in all things your masters according to the flesh; not with eyeservice, as menpleasers; but in singleness of heart, fearing God: And whatsoever ye do, do it heartily, as to the Lord, and not unto men."* Regarding this passage, I simply want to focus on the phrase "singleness of heart" and the word "heartily". In scripture, the heart is often termed as the seat of one's emotions and passions. It can drive the whole being. You see, it is one thing to "put your mind" to something and another entirely to "put your heart" to it.

For example, I have witnessed many great piano players and have often heard different pianists play the same songs. Though one might be inclined to say that there is no difference in their styles, when you see a piano player not just play with his mental capability, but also with the capacity of his heart, somehow the song becomes more alive and touching.

What Paul meant by "singleness of heart" was that the Christian is called to serve with heartfelt sincerity. There is to be genuineness to what we do and to who we are. I grow tired of believers who still put on facades with one another, simply because they would rather "appear" holy than sincere. We are called to confess our faults with one another and bear each others burdens, not wear a mask!

Now, lets move on to the word "heartily". This does not necessarily mean being jovial, though we are to "rejoice in the Lord always", but it refers to the call that whatever you do, do it from the depths of your soul to the Lord. It is very similar to when people say, "From the bottom of my heart." Scraping the bottom of the barrel may yield very little, but when one serves from the bottom of their heart, they will find lasting unction.

Finally, Jesus said, *"For where your treasure is, there will your heart be also* (Luke 12:34)." People sometimes say of a daydreamer, "His body may be here, but his mind is elsewhere." For the Christian, he is to have sincerity and unction in his life, but all of this stems from having his heart occupied with the life and love of Jesus Christ. Your body may be here on earth, but your heart is to be in heaven, enthroned with the presence of Christ. There are some that though trials are all around them, their joy is not crushed because it is tucked away in the One Who will never fail or forsake them.

FOR TODAY
Read

Colossians 3 (Morning)
If verses 18-21 refer to our behavior within the home, what does the call of verses 12-17 speak to?

1 Corinthians 10:23-33 (Noon)
Can you think of an example of where a believer might be offensive to another, even though what he is doing is not necessarily wrong?

John 4 (Night)
What did Jesus mean when He said in verse thirty two, "I have meat to eat ye know not of"?

Perhaps we do less Actions, for He is not more adored. Cherish Jesus and you'll have no problem laboring for the kingdom

Day 13

In the King James Version, Psalms 68:19 states, *"Blessed be the Lord, who daily loadeth us with benefits, even the God of our salvation. Selah."* Sometimes I look into other translations for a broader and better understanding of a passage. What is interesting is that, in the original Hebrew, this verse in particular is a little ambiguous. "With benefits" is not directly stated in the passage; therefore, the translators put it in italics. This verse has a beautiful promise of the blessings of God, but what I find even more amazing is what other translations reveal regarding verse 19.

Now, before I quote the *Young's Literal Translation,* one must understand that this is a barebones version. By this I mean that it translates a passage as it is directly stated in Hebrew and Greek. Normally, it does not "butter up" a verse to make it more palatable to the understanding. So with this knowledge, let's look at what it states, *"Blessed is the Lord, day by day He layeth on us. God Himself is our salvation. Selah."* The implication in this verse is that God "lays upon us" Himself, or more accurately, His presence is in the midst of His people. This is entirely true as well, for the wonderful presence of God is always over His children, guiding and protecting.

The next version I will list is the LITV or *The Literal Translation Version.* Though this may sound similar to Young's Literal, it gives a more "polished" translation to make is easier to comprehend. Psalms 68:19 is stated as, *"Blessed be the Lord: day by day He carries a load for us, the God of our salvation. Selah."* So, we went from Provisions in the KJV, to Presence in the YLT, and finally Peace in the LITV. What do I mean by this? Notice, that this verse states that God "carries a load for us." He can bear the infirmities and hardships of His children, giving us peace and comfort where once we felt "heavy laden."

David declared in Psalms 55:22a, *"Cast thy burden upon the LORD, and he shall sustain thee..."*

Someone may say, "Wait! These verses are contradictory!" However, this is not true. No matter the translation of this verse it still conveys the promises of God that are affirmed all throughout scripture. I prefer the King James Version in which we can rejoice because God does "daily load us with benefits/blessings." Yet, I rejoice in the other translations as well, because I know that God's presence is undeniably near and many times He will take away my burdens, giving me peace. Simply, I embrace all three truths with great joy! Perhaps, you should too.

FOR TODAY
Read

Psalms 68 (Morning)
What is verse 18 prophetic of? Hint: Ephesians 4:8

Psalms 55:12-23 (Noon)
What is the hopeful promise that David gives in verses 22?
Look up
1 Peter 5:6-7 as well.

Psalms 116 (Night)
Mark the statements where David affirms, "I will". These are heartfelt commitments. Meditate on them and with an honest heart think about what commitments God desires you to make.

The Vision of the American Church is like a man preoccupied with killing a fly, while driving 100 miles an hour on winding roads. We must get our focus back on God's purpose, relinquishing our petty squabbles and prejudices that hold us back from true, spiritual power

Day 14

Isaiah 55:1 states, *"Ho* (or Pay attention!), *every one that thirsteth, come ye to the waters, and he that hath no money; come ye, buy, and eat; yea, come, buy wine and milk without money and without price."* Jesus declared in Matthew 11:28, *"Come unto me, all ye that labour and are heavy laden, and I will give you rest."* In the last chapter of the Bible, through the Holy Spirit's leading, John wrote, *"And the Spirit and the bride say, Come. And let him that heareth say, Come. And let him that is athirst come. And whosoever will, let him take the water of life freely.* (Revelation 22:17)."

All throughout scripture, God's call to us has been the same, "COME UNTO ME." It is the gospel message, a glorious invitation to freely receive salvation! To think that the Lord of the universe would bid me a lowly sinner to come to Him, sit at His feet, and partake of His abundant grace is beyond my understanding!

Yet, God longs for us to come that we might experience His love and see His goodness. In Psalms 34:8, David joyously wrote, *"O taste and see that the LORD is good: blessed is the man that trusteth in him."* Have you truly tasted of the goodness and grace of God? We use our mouths to taste. In the same way, it is through our mouths that we taste of God's grace, because Paul stated in Romans 10:10, *"For with the heart man believeth unto righteousness; and with the mouth confession is made unto salvation."*

God is calling all of humanity to come back to Him and partake in the banquet of redemption (Isaiah 55:1-2). This is done when we confess and repent of our sins and open our hearts to receive His love! Again, I ask, have you truly tasted of the goodness and grace of God? The gift of salvation is free, but to receive it means you are to let go of the sin you cling onto. Jesus revealed that many will not COME to the light, because they do not want their sins to be exposed (John 3:20). Those who eat at the table of grace acknowledge that they are hungry, undeserving beggars.

Again, God is calling out "Come unto Me." You can partake in His goodness, but you must acknowledge your need of Him, confess your sins, and trust Christ as Lord. I leave you with this thought – A person that will not let go of his sins is like a skydiver who won't let go of a shiny bowling ball, so he can open the parachute.

FOR TODAY
Read

Isaiah 55 (Morning)
What is the assurance we have been given concerning God's Word in this passage?

Matthew 11:20-30 and 23:34-39 (Noon)

Luke 18 (Night)
Though Christ is calling "come unto me", what does verse 14 tell us about those who live in religious pride? (Look up James 4:6)

The skeptic spends most of his time slandering, not seeking. He spends much time learning new ways to argue. He holds to deceitful opinions rather than honest facts. If only he took as much effort to study God's truth and learn of "the reason of hope that lies within us," perhaps he would find his heart and mind pointing to one fact: Jesus is the Savior of the world

Day 15

There are many people who can easily quote John 3:16. This verse is embedded into fabrics like T-Shirts and Ties, placed in quaint picture frames and Christian posters, and often used on religious billboards and signs. Yet, for all the "knowledge" of God's love, there are less and less people experiencing and sharing His love in this world. The reality is that anyone can quote scripture until they are blue in the face, but until God's Word penetrates the understanding of the mind and the passion of the heart, it profits little.

The depth of words is often lost in today's society. For example, the word *"believe"* has been used so many times with the sappy statement, *"Believe in yourself"* that it now bears a watered down connotation. It is a little pinch of trust mixed with good feelings. So for some people when they hear a person say, *"Believe in Jesus,"* it is almost like hearing Peter Pan declare, *"Think happy thoughts!"* Undeniably, happy thoughts will not transform the wickedness of the heart.

In light of this, we must ask ourselves, what does it scripturally mean for one to believe in Jesus? The Greek word for believe implies a continual, concrete trust in someone or something. In salvation, it goes deeper to continually entrusting one's entire being and welfare to Jesus Christ (1 Peter 4:19). Paul expounds even further on salvation and believing in Christ, when he wrote, *"That if thou shalt confess with thy mouth the Lord Jesus, and shalt believe in thine heart that God hath raised him from the dead, thou shalt be saved.* (Romans 10:9)"

The notes in the Geneva Bible Translation sums up the meaning of "confess" well by stating, "If you profess plainly, sincerely, and openly..." Believing in Christ entails that outwardly we honestly and unashamedly acknowledge Him as our Savior and inwardly we enthrone Him as our Lord. It is where we give Him full reign over our lives, while renouncing all other influences. He alone is to be the ruler of our hearts.

Also, such belief encompasses trusting that Jesus rose again. This is so crucial! Notice what Peter says in 1 Peter 1:3, *"Praise the God and Father of our Lord Jesus Christ! God has given us a new birth because of his great mercy. We have been born into a new life that has a confidence which is alive because Jesus Christ has come back to life. (GWT)"* My faith, hope, and joy rests in the resurrection power of Christ. Praise God Jesus is alive and His Spirit is living in me! This is true Christian belief.

FOR TODAY
Read

Romans 10 (Morning)
Why do you think so many seek to "establish their own righteousness (vs. 3)?"

Psalms 40:1-3 (Noon)
Meditate on these verses and think about how they are descriptive of salvation

Deuteronomy 30 (Night)
What did Moses mean by his statement regarding the heart in verse 6? Look up Colossians 2:11

Sadly, there are many careless souls who have superficially confessed Christ with their mouth, but are still solidly condemned in their heart

Day 16

Very often in the book of Psalms, the word *Selah,* pronounced as sea-law, is mentioned. This is because it is a musical notation that introduces a moment of refrain. Literally, it is a pause; a suspended silence that can cause one to meditate upon what was previously sung and written.

For example, even though Psalms chapter 3 only has 8 verses, *Selah* is used 3 times with the final verse declaring, *"Salvation belongeth unto the LORD: thy blessing is upon thy people. Selah."* Take some time to read this Psalm. The first two verses are a desperate prayer for deliverance, ending with *Selah.* The next two are an affirmation of God's power and care, and again, *Selah.* The final verses are rejoicing in God's salvation and blessings over His people. And of course, *Selah* is the final word stated. It's as if every musical suspension seemed to propel David's confidence back in God.

Now some may think, "What does this matter? Why should one word make a difference?" *Selah* is much more than a musical term, it is a call for every believer! What do I mean by this? All of us need moments of refrain, rest, and reflection. We are so busy with work and investing in worldly pursuits that we almost never stop to simply rejoice in God's goodness. Perhaps it is because when we do pause, we see our lives for what they are, anemic and powerless. It is magnified that we were spiritually running on fumes, neglecting the power of God's Spirit.

Regarding the foolishness of the children of Israel in the wilderness, the Psalmist writes, *"They soon forgat his works; they waited not for his counsel: But lusted exceedingly in the wilderness, and tested God in the desert* (Psalms 106:13).*"* How did they come to "forget" God and His works? In his commentary, Adam Clarke says, "They were impatient, and would not wait till God should in his own way fulfill his own designs." It was because they did not take time to wait on God and meditate on His Word! It is so imperative that each day we have a *"Selah"* time; A pause in life where we can sit at the feet of Jesus and feast on His Word. God said in Psalms 46:10, *"Be still, and know that I am God: I will be exalted among the heathen, I will be exalted in the earth."* Sometimes the best thing we can do in life is just be still and stand in awe of Him.

FOR TODAY

Read

Psalms 46 (Morning)
Why could the Psalmist say that he would not fear even if the mountains crumble into the sea?

Psalms 4 and Mark 4:35-41 (Noon)
Has there ever been a time in your life, when you have let worries and fears cause you to think the way the disciples did in verse 38?

2 Chronicles 20 (Night)
Before a seemingly impossible battle, what did the Israelites do (Vs. 15-22)?

James said that with some people you will have to pull them out of the fire, hating even the garment spotted by the flesh. So, how can we not be burned in reaching out to others? Learn the lesson of the 3 Hebrew children. The closer you are to Christ, the more you can take the world's heat and come away unharmed. Sadly, this is why so many do not reach out to those in bondage, for they are not immersed in the Water of Life

Day 17

I have often heard people say, "Time flies, when you're having fun." I am sure that you would agree with me that it doesn't matter whether you are "having fun" or not, time simply appears to be flying by faster and faster with each new day. I remember when I was seven, I mailed off several proof of purchases from cereal boxes to get a special toy. The problem was that I had to wait a full three weeks for processing and delivery. It felt like ages then. Now, as a working adult with three children, three weeks feels like three days!

A retired elderly man once told me, "Right now you are on roller skates, but wait till you get my age. You will feel like life is as fast as a rocket ship." Somewhere between the transitioning of youth to adulthood, there is a startling realization that time is not a friend and life is short. The apostle James wrote, *"Whereas ye know not what shall be on the morrow. For what is your life? It is even a vapour, that appeareth for a little time, and then vanisheth away. (James 4:14)"* Truly, our lives are like a single snowflake that falls onto black asphalt in the midst of a sunny day.

Some people believe that once a person dies, they cease to exist. Man becomes oblivion. Yet, the Bible teaches, *"...it is appointed unto men once to die, but after this the judgment.* (Hebrews 9:27)" The writer of Hebrews states again in chapter 13 and verse 14, *"We don't have a permanent city here on earth, but we are looking for the city that we will have in the future.* (GWT)" This life is not the end of the story. There is so much more! So, life on earth is not just some melting snowflake, but is also a colorful dot on a massive, beautiful canvas.

However, such news should give us not only joy, but also reverential fear, because there is a coming judgment. 2

Corinthians 5:10 states, *"For we must all appear before the judgment seat of Christ; that every one may receive the things done in his body, according to that he hath done, whether it be good or bad."* You see, we have hope that death is not the end, and what is done in this life can make an eternal impact. Everyday is a chance to "redeem the time"; to make a difference in someone's life and for the kingdom of God. Let's not squander opportunities to show Christ's love or spend all of our time investing in temporal amusements and decaying possessions. Let's keep our hearts glancing at eternity as we walk from day to day. We will soon see that everyday we follow God's Spirit is another colorful mark imprinted on the canvas of eternity.

FOR TODAY
Read

Psalms 90 (Morning)
Because of the brevity of life, what did Moses pray for (vs. 12-17)?

Psalms 39 (Noon)
What is the "best" man has to offer?

James 4 (Night)
What are the implications of verse 15, when it comes to every day life?

The Danger in much Labor is growing Distant in Love. Take time to simply rest in His power and grace

Day 18

When I was a child, my dad was in the Navy. In just a few years, we moved from Florida to Louisiana to Texas, and finally to North Carolina. Even in NC, for financial reasons, my family moved three other times before finally "settling down". I was about thirteen, when we stopped moving. In between those years, I said goodbye to a lot of friends, lost several pets, my grandfather died, and my parents divorced. Life is not an easy road nor is it predictable. Many times in ministry I have seen children and teens alike living most of their lives in an unstable environment.

Even when there is a mother and father within the home, there are so many "other" things vying for one's attention, that there's a great disconnect between the parents and their kids. So the question is raised, where can one find the place where peacefulness and security dwell? David confidently wrote in Psalms 27, "*I have asked one thing from the LORD. This I will seek: to remain in the LORD'S house all the days of my life in order to gaze at the LORD'S beauty and to search for an answer in his temple. He hides me in his shelter when there is trouble. He keeps me hidden in his tent. He sets me high on a rock.....{When you said,} "Seek my face," my heart said to you, "O LORD, I will seek your face".....Even if my father and mother abandon me, the LORD will take care of me* (4-5, 8, 10 /GWT)."

Stability is found only through seeking God. The death of my granddad and the divorce of my parents happened in the same year. My mother would tell me often that I always had a Heavenly Father. It wasn't long after those tragic events that I received the Life and Love of Jesus in my heart! It has often been said, "Home is where the heart is", but I would say that home is where Jesus dwells. Praise the Lord that every child, every adult, every person who trusts in and seeks after Jesus will find stability and peace.

The apostle John prophesied in Revelation 21:1, 3-4, *"And I saw a new heaven and a new earth: for the first heaven and the first earth were passed away; and there was no more sea...And I heard a great voice out of heaven saying, Behold, the tabernacle of God is with men, and he will dwell with them, and they shall be his people, and God himself shall be with them, and be their God. And God shall wipe away all tears from their eyes; and there shall be no more death, neither sorrow, nor crying, neither shall there be any more pain: for the former things are passed away."* His presence is our Home and one day we will experience the fullness of what it means to have an eternal home with Him. To this I write, just as John did, "even so, come, Lord Jesus."

FOR TODAY
Read

Psalms 27 (Morning)
What strong affirmation does David end his Psalm with?

John 15:1-11 (Noon)

Isaiah 25 (Night)
How does verse 8 correlate with the teaching in Revelation 7 and 21?

The best way we can read the Bible is read it prayerfully (pray for wisdom and guidance), persistently (make it a daily habit), passionately (desire it), and purposefully (read to get something out of it)*

40

Day 19

In the first chapter of the Gospel of Luke, Gabriel, an angel of the Lord, appears to a priest named Zechariah, declaring that though he and his wife were old, they would have a son. His son's name would be called John. In the midst of such joyous news, Zechariah questioned the validity of such a miracle. Thus, Gabriel chided him for his unbelief and pronounced that he would be mute until his son was born (I'm sure Zechariah's wife didn't mind that!). What is interesting is that you will find in the same chapter, Gabriel appearing to Mary, telling her how she would have a child named Jesus. Mary as well questioned how this could happen because she had not been with any man. He simply tells her that it would be a work of the Holy Spirit.

Now, for those who are familiar with this chapter, they may have oftentimes questioned why Zechariah was chided and stuck with not being able to speak, while Mary faced no severe verdict. Perhaps it was because Zechariah was a man, right? When one delves deeper into the responses of Zechariah & Mary, he will understand why this happened exactly as it did. We will first examine Zechariah's response. Luke 1:11-13 states, *"And there appeared unto him an angel of the Lord standing on the right side of the altar of incense. And when Zacharias saw him, he was troubled, and fear fell upon him. But the angel said unto him, Fear not, Zacharias: for thy prayer is heard; and thy wife Elisabeth shall bear thee a son, and thou shalt call his name John."*

First, we must realize that Zechariah was a priest. He was not some common fisherman or a lowly shepherd. His position held great accountability. Naturally, he would teach to others of the power and wonders of God. He studied and believed in the miracle of Isaac given to Abraham & Sarah, and yet he did not believe the angel of the Lord that stood directly before him!

41

Secondly, notice that he had already been praying for a child for sometime! The angel said, *"...for thy prayer is heard."* Sadly, this reminds me of times when I have prayed for something, but deep down did not believe God would answer. When He would answer my request, I would toss it aside as coincidence.

Finally, we see the depth of Zechariah's doubt when he says, *"Whereby shall I know this? for I am an old man, and my wife well stricken in years."* Literally, he asked for a sign! He wanted the angel to give him some prepackaged proof and boy the angel did just that. For nine months, Elizabeth, Zechariah's wife, won every marital "discussion". Lord willing, tomorrow we will look closer into Mary's response, which will reveal a response we all need to learn and imitate.

FOR TODAY
Read

Luke 1:1-25 (Morning)
What was the purpose of Luke's writing (vs. 1-4)?

Genesis 18:1-14 (Noon)

Hebrews 11 (Night)
In verse 6, what are the two essentials in "coming to God"?

Our society bellows forth the hope of 'finding yourself' in life as if when you realize who you are, everything is complete. Yet, Jesus taught that we must lose our lives, if we are to find true, abundant life. We do not need to be asking the question who am I, but only to get lost in the wonder of Who He is

Day 20

Yesterday, you would have read about Zechariah's response to the angel Gabriel who promised him that though his wife was of great age, she would have a son. It is evident in Luke 1 that his heart was blinded by unbelief, thus Gabriel declared that he would be mute until the child was born. Now, let us focus on Mary, the mother of Jesus. The same chapter that reveals Zechariah's reaction also reveals Mary's response to Gabriel telling her that she would have a child named Jesus, though she had not been with a man. Mary as well wondered over such news stating, *"How shall this be, seeing I know not a man?"* (Luke 1:34)

On the surface, it would appear that Mary's reaction was similar to that of Zechariah's, but nothing could be farther from the truth. In yesterday's article, we have already seen how Zechariah was a priest who was held up to a higher accountability and how he had already been praying for a child. Yet, when given news that he was to have a son, he seeks for a sign of proof!

As we look deeper in Luke 1, we will see the true, steadfast faith Mary had in God. First, we must realize that at this time she was already betrothed to Joseph - this carries a much more serious meaning than what we view an "engagement" today as – and she was a virgin, saving herself for when their marriage was complete. Naturally, she would question how she could have a child. Zechariah had the testimony of Abraham and Sarah, who had Isaac at a ripe, old age but no one had ever heard of a virgin bearing a child!

Mary's own plans of married life seemed to be snatched out from under her. She knew that it would be nearly impossible for Joseph to believe such news and she also knew that, if he did not, she could face abandonment from family, persecution, and ultimately death. However, once Gabriel reminded and affirmed to her that "nothing is impossible with God," notice Mary's remarkable response, *"Behold the handmaid of the Lord; be it unto me according to thy word."* (Luke 1:38)

Complete surrender. She wholly committed herself to the will of God. We may wonder sometimes how God may work through someone or in a certain situation, but never doubt that He will do what He says He is going to do! Simply, like Mary, be available to all the He is, willing to say, "be it unto me according to Thy Word!" If you would live out such an attitude each day, you'll find the Christian walk much more adventurous and delightful, and yes, even miraculous.

FOR TODAY
Read

Luke 1:26-80 (Morning)
Meditate on Mary's praise to the Lord. What did Zechariah do right after the birth of his son?

Psalms 37:1-11 (Noon)
In these verses, highlight key words such as "Fret not" & "Trust."

Isaiah 6 (Night)
After his revelation and repentance, what was Isaiah's response to the call of God?

Remember that a new day means newness in your Christian walk. Do not make every opportunity "count", but make every opportunity Christ-like

Day 21

I remember many years ago when I first began Driver's Education, I was so nervous over the thought of getting into an accident that I wouldn't say a word to anyone in the car for fear of distraction. When driving, I was watchful (or you could say "edgy") and I tried to be attentive to any sound that resembled sirens, horns, and screeching tires. To be honest, I was probably a little too cautious.

Obviously, now that I have been driving for many years, my "nervousness" of the road has drastically diminished. I am certain that this is the case for so many people on the road. There is a sense of confidence and also a little bit of ignorance exercised every time we drive our vehicles. We have confidence in our experience but ignorance that we don't think about how, if we're not careful, that drive could be our last.

One thing we must consider is that if there is a need to be alert on the road, how much more are we to be vigilant in our day to day walk as a Christian? In his first epistle, Peter urged believers to, *"Be sober, be vigilant; because your adversary the devil, as a roaring lion, walketh about, seeking whom he may devour."* (1 Peter 5:8) In a similar way, Paul revealed to the Christians at Corinth that they should not be overly confident by thinking they are "untouchable." He wrote, *"Wherefore let him that thinketh he standeth take heed lest he fall."* (1 Corinthians 10:12)

If the devil can't have your soul, then through amusement or busyness, he will seek to distract you from serving God. He will hurl at you many temptations, so that your personal walk with God is deteriorated to a formality or a trite fancy. Many of us have been lulled to sleep with legalism, forgetting that it is through the grace of God that we are taught to deny *"ungodliness and worldly lusts."* (Titus 2:12) When we begin to truly see the wonders of God's grace, it presses us on to live for Him. For some, they have "fallen" into sin and are duped into believing that this backwards living is "real life" and hardly inescapable.

We were made for so much more! We are redeemed to bear fruit! In 1 Corinthians 10:13, Paul reminded the believers of God's faithfulness in their lives by writing, *"There hath no temptation taken you but such as is common to man: but God is faithful, who will not suffer you to be tempted above that ye are able; but will with the temptation also make a way to escape, that ye may be able to bear it."* We can overcome sin, through the power and grace of God. Love God, Study His Word, pray often and always be spiritually alert.

FOR TODAY
Read

Luke 22 (Morning)

What did Jesus urge the disciples to do in the garden of Gesthemane (Matthew 26:41)?

Romans 13:8-14 (Noon)
In this passage, what are Christians called to "put on"?

1 Thessalonians 5 (Night)
Similar to the noon question, describe the "armor" that Paul calls all believers to put on.

The wicked inventions of the mind, if not cast down by the Word of God, will infect your heart and then infiltrate your actions

Day 22

1 Thessalonians 1:4-7 states, *"For we know, brothers loved by God, that he has chosen you, because our gospel came to you not only in word, but also in power and in the Holy Spirit and with full conviction. You know what kind of men we proved to be among you for your sake. And you became imitators of us and of the Lord, for you received the word in much affliction, with the joy of the Holy Spirit, so that you became an example to all the believers in Macedonia and in Achaia* (ESV)."

If there is one thing I have realized about this generation of young people it is that, in the midst of a society of uncertainty and extreme tolerance, still somehow they can easily spot a "fake" a mile away. They seek genuineness within the church that is so often lacking. At times I have met university students who knew little of the Bible, but still perceived that there were many double standards within the American church. I understand that the "hypocrisy" bit is many times a copout to not attend worship services, but this simple accusation should not be ignored. We must dig deep and begin to see that perhaps we have become "WORD ONLY" Christians.

There are many, including myself, who have declared, "Oh if only things were like it was years ago!" However, the older I get and the more I hear of what church was like in the "golden years," the more I realize that church was simply a social norm which extended no further than the pews. It was commonplace, so one did not need to have a hunger for God as long as he "tipped his hat" to Him each week. Over time, we have traded empowering faith for empty, rote fundamentalism.

We have tricked ourselves into thinking that the world is to come into the church, rather than the church go out into the world. In many ways, we have set aside the will and workings of the Holy Spirit. Oh that all Christians today would become genuine, yielded vessels so that the power of the Holy Spirit would flow through them! If only we didn't just speak Christianity, but demonstrated it fully through our actions, our attitude, and our aspirations. It is then that the church would become *"an example to all believers"* and a true light to the world.

FOR TODAY
Read

Ephesians 5 (Morning)
What should never be exemplified in a Christian's life (vs. 3-4)?
How is the believer to "walk" in this life?

Matthew 6:1-13 (Noon)
What would be an example of idle talk or "vain repetitions?"

Acts 19 (Night)
Why could not the travelling Jews cast out demons?

****I could place the prettiest pictures with passionate Christian phrases and quotes on my wall, but if Christ is not placed on the throne of my heart, what good is it?***

Day 23

Paul writes in the later part of 2 Corinthians 10:12, *"...they measuring themselves by themselves, and comparing themselves among themselves, are not wise."* Many times, when I have talked to someone about their sin and need of God's forgiveness, they say to me, "Well preacher, at least I'm not like this guy!" I remember, on one occasion, I even had to listen to a mother say, "Bro. Josh, my son may be a drunk but at least he hasn't murdered anyone." It seems that as long as we can pinpoint someone that has done worse things than us somehow it makes everything a little better for our standing in life. Is your integrity questionable? Simply, find someone with a lot more dirt under his boots and your character will look that much more appealing. This may be the American way, but understand that this most certainly is not the Christian way.

Our lives are not to be compared with other people's faults and problems. We are to live by the Word of God, the same scriptures that the apostle James says is like a mirror. The Law of God reveals the knowledge of sin in our own lives. Let a little boy go outside for a couple hours and what will eventually happen? He may get some cuts or bruises, but he would definitely get dirty and no matter how many times you tell to him, "You're filthy! Come inside and get clean." It is only when you scoop him up, take him inside, and sit him in front of a mirror that he sees how dirty he really is.

I have two simple questions, how long has it been since you sat down and looked into the mirror of God's precious Word? Has all your time been spent comparing yourself to others rather than committing yourself to God's Truth? Praise the Lord that the Bible not only exposes our mistakes and failures, but also magnifies Christ's sustaining grace. Paul goes on to write in chapter ten, *"But he that glorieth, let him glory in the Lord. For not he that commendeth himself is approved, but whom the Lord commendeth. (17-18)."*

Two of the biggest mistakes I have made in trying to somehow "certify" my faithfulness to God is when I have tried to compare myself to others and what they do; and when I have exalted my past achievements, as if they were enough to vouch for my present commitment. In your Christian walk, don't be fooled with the attitude "Well, at least I'm better than so and so." Do not be blinded with past successes that you end up tossing aside future opportunities to glorify God. We have nothing to boast and glory in except in the Lord, Jesus Christ! Proverbs 20:6 states, *"Most men will proclaim every one his own goodness: but a faithful man who can find?"* Christianity is not about making yourself look good by ridiculing the faults of others. It is about seeking to glorify God by resting in and rejoicing over His grace.

FOR TODAY
Read

1 Thessalonians 2 (Morning)
What type of character did Paul live out towards the Thessalonian believers?

Psalms 34 (Noon)

Psalms 71 (Night)
Even at an old age, David did not excuse himself from being faithful to the work of the Lord. What was his prayer and aim (vs. 17-18)?

Those who pray little, do not make much of God, nor do much for Him

Day 24

Proverbs 25:11 declares, *"A word fitly spoken is like apples of gold in pictures of silver,"* and Proverbs 15:23 states, *"A man hath joy by the answer of his mouth: and a word spoken in due season, how good is it!"* Over the years, there have been many people I have met who seemed to know exactly what to say, when I was going through a personal trial. Their words of wisdom and comfort may not have been the most eloquent or the most elaborate, but they were priceless to me. On the other hand, I have equally met some who have caused me to be discouraged and my heart troubled with just a few words spoken in bitterness. Just as several kind words can greatly uplift the spirit, words spoken in anger or criticism can diminish one's hope and hurt the soul. Proverbs 15:4 says, *"A wholesome tongue is a tree of life: but perverseness therein is a breach in the spirit."* It is a sad fact, yet often the people that wield the greatest pain to Christians are not vigorous atheists or even haters of religion, but professed believers as well! Some of the worst quarrelling can be found in the church pew just as easily as in the trailer park. It almost always begins with one foolish statement spoken in pride or anger.

Why is it that, for so many Christians, their lingo seems to bear no difference to the World's? I believe it is because there are two important truths which are easily overlooked regarding the Christian life. First, the call to love one another has been dimmed in our hearts. Paul wrote in Galatians 5:13-15, *"For, brethren, ye have been called unto liberty; only use not liberty for an occasion to the flesh, but by love serve one another. For all the law is fulfilled in one word, even in this; Thou shalt love thy neighbour as thyself. But if ye bite and devour one another, take heed that ye be not consumed one of another."* We can certainly "bite, devour, and consume" each other by the contemptible words we say and the bitter attitudes we express.

It may seem extreme, but I often term heated church conflicts as Spiritual Cannibalism. Someone who is focused on and filled with the love of God will not "lie to or lash out at" his fellow man.

Another reason our speech may bear little godly testimony is because we have forgotten the accountability we are under. Jesus said, *"... every idle word that men shall speak, they shall give account thereof in the day of judgment. For by thy words thou shalt be justified, and by thy words thou shalt be condemned* (Matthew 12:36-37). " In the Greek, "idle" means careless, lazy, and useless. I shudder to think of things I have said in anger, let alone words spoken haphazardly! We must realize that our words are important and it's not just about what we say but how we say it. Ask God to give you wisdom to know when to speak and when not to. Pray that His love and grace would overflow from your heart, to your lips, and mightily impact those you speak to from day to day. *"Everything you say should be kind and well thought out so that you know how to answer everyone* (Colossians 4:6, God's Word Translation)."

FOR TODAY
Read

Proverbs 15 (Morning)
How does verse 4 and Proverbs 18:21 correlate?

Colossians 4:1-6 & Titus 2:1-8 (Noon)

James 3 (Night)
List some of the depictions given regarding the tongue and what point does James make as to why we do not curse others (vs. 9)?

Be quick to bow your knees and slow to raise your fist

Day 25

Paul wrote in Colossians 1:27, *"To whom God would make known what is the riches of the glory of this mystery among the Gentiles; which is Christ in you, the hope of glory."* I believe that if you took every aspect of the Christian life, every doctrine and truth, it could be summed up in this one statement, *"Christ in you, the hope of glory."* Christ in me? What a paradox! When we think of the gospel message, we often think of telling people about heaven and how they can go. However, the gospel is not just news about the God who wants people to go to heaven. It is much greater, even better than this fact. The gospel message is about the God who wants to get back into the person, so that He might *"work in him mightily"* on earth to do His will and accomplish His purpose, which is ultimately to glorify Himself! Now we are getting somewhere.

I know of some Christians who believe the only way to be holy is to muse over Christ's example on earth and to strive to imitate His teachings. They equate strenuous activity with holiness. How many times do we fall under the same guise of "speedy sanctification", when all the while, we feel empty inside and even more unholy? If we are not careful, we can easily forget the wonderful truth that Christ is in us! Is He inactive, while we labor till we drop? Does He on one side give us a home in heaven, and on the other side tell us that we must "fend" for ourselves on earth, if we are to please God? The answer is a resounding NO.

Let us see what Paul teaches in two of his epistles. First, Paul writes in Galatians 2:20, *"I am crucified with Christ: nevertheless I live; yet not I, but Christ liveth in me: and the life which I now live in the flesh I live by the faith of the Son of God, who loved me, and gave himself for me."* Second, in Philippians 1:21, Paul states, *"For to me to live is Christ, and to die is*

53

gain." Notice the phrases, "*Christ liveth in me*", and "*For to me to live is Christ.*" Christ's power not only frees us from sin, but His life in us enables us to truly live! He came to give us "*life more abundantly.*"

We must have faith that He has not only saved us, but also that He is presently living through us! Sometimes, in our day to day activity, we need to stop and simply pray, "Jesus, I'm sorry that I have let my body, heart, and mind get ahead of your life and your Father's will. I surrender. Live in me the life that I cannot live myself, so that your work will be accomplished and God will be glorified." Never forget verse 29 of Colossians chapter 1, "*Whereunto I also labor, striving according to his working which worketh in me mightily.*"

FOR TODAY
Read

Colossians 1:1-12 & 2 Corinthians 5:12-21 (Morning)
What was Paul's prayer for the Christians in Colosse (vs. 9-12)?

Ezekiel 36:22-38 (Noon)
How would the Isrealites "walk in (God's) statutes"?

1 Corinthians 1 (Night)
Jesus is "made unto us" what (vs. 30)?

I have no true power until I am crucified within, and I serve no true purpose until I seek to edify without

Day 26

During a time of prayer and study, I came across the well known verse Psalms 118:24 that declares, "*This is the day which the LORD hath made; we will rejoice and be glad in it.*" I have read and sung this verse over a hundred times, yet it is certain that through the revealing of God's Spirit, His Word is alive and its treasures are not limited to a one time reading. As I began to think over this passage, my heart burst with delight and my eyes with tears. Why? Notice the promise, "*This is the day.*" What day, or more accurately, Who's day? It may seem cliché, but it is God's day. Paul said in Romans 14:5-6a & 7-8, "*One man esteemeth one day above another: another esteemeth every day alike. Let every man be fully persuaded in his own mind. He that regardeth the day, regardeth it unto the Lord; and he that regardeth not the day, to the Lord he doth not regard it...For none of us liveth to himself, and no man dieth to himself. For whether we live, we live unto the Lord; and whether we die, we die unto the Lord: whether we live therefore, or die, we are the Lord's.*"

Often, upon experiencing a trial or facing disappointment, I have heard people say (I am in this group as well), "This just isn't my day." Well, they are right. No day is. We are given an invitation to dance in creation's song, but we cannot control its rhythm. We begin to find the beauty of harmonic grace, when we acknowledge everyday as a day unto the Lord. Even more, the Psalmist declared that this is the day which the LORD has made. Do we truly realize that our tomorrows have already been sifted through the hands of God? That nothing has blindsided Him today, there is grace sufficient, and victory assured, because He has "made it." We can boldly claim 1 Thessalonians 5:24, "*Faithful is He that calleth you, who also will do it,*" for if He made today, how dare we think that it carries with it far too many surprises for us, and far too many issues for God to redeem it for His glory. Every day, every hour, every second is in His hands. I needed to be reminded, once again, that there is Purpose, there is Protection, and there is Power in each moment.

In light of this, our call is to rejoice and be glad in each day. This bears the same truth that Paul wrote in 1Thessalonnians 5:18, "*In every thing give thanks: for this is the will of God in Christ Jesus concerning you*", and Philippians 4:4, "*Rejoice in the Lord alway: and again I say, Rejoice.*" The OT word for "rejoice" literally means to "spin wildly." It's not just from the mind to the mouth. No, somehow the understanding that in TODAY there is a lavish supply of grace and forgiveness, love and power, peace and joy, should make its way to our hearts and overflow. Simply, do you BELIEVE that "This is the day which the LORD hath made", and in this grand assurance, will you "rejoice and be glad in it."

FOR TODAY
Read

Psalms 118 (Morning)
Verses 22-23 is spoken of in Matthew 21:42, Mark 12:10, Luke 20:17, Acts 4:11, & 1 Peter 2:7. Who is it referring to?

Romans 14:1-8 (Noon)

Ephesians 2 (Night)
It is by grace through faith that we are saved, yet in verse 10, what did Paul remind the believers concerning God's plan?

If you pray like no one is listening, then you will receive like no one is giving

Day 27

At the beginning of Psalms 42:5, the psalmist gives an interesting description of depression by stating, *"Why art thou cast down, O my soul? and why art thou disquieted in me?"* "Cast down" is mentioned 4 times in chapters 42 and 43. It means to sink low or to depress. "Disquieted" is recorded 3 times implying a great commotion and struggle within the soul. Have you ever felt this way? On the outside, we may appear mildly discouraged, but inwardly there is a storm raging. Often I have heard people say, upon just finding out that a loved one battled with depression, "I never knew they were hurting. They never showed it." If we are not careful, we can easily look over the soul pains of another. We must come to terms with the fact that we live in a world of heartache, so to brush under the carpet the reality of this psychological anxiety and spiritual struggle would be a grave mistake.

No one is immune to it. It is a universal thorn which can prick any heart through fears, failures, and even by feelings. Depression is a street that satan desires everyone to travel down. Why? In all seriousness, it is because the road of depression will eventually lead one to a dead end. Jesus said in John 10:10, *"The thief cometh not, but for to steal, and to kill, and to destroy: I am come that they might have life, and that they might have it more abundantly."* Satan wants nothing more than to keep people away from an abundant life in Jesus Christ.

What can we do when we are faced with such sorrowful struggles or when we know someone else who is hurting within? First, let us go back to Verse 5 of Psalms 42. The writer began with a question as to why he was "cast down", but he ends with an affirmation of joy. Here is the verse in its entirety, *"Why art thou cast down, O my soul? and why art thou disquieted in me? hope thou in God: for I shall yet praise him for the help of his countenance. . " The* devil's arrow of despair can never penetrate our hearts, when we are exercising faith and hope in God.

The psalmist will go on to proclaim in Psalms 42:7–8, *"Deep calleth unto deep at the noise of thy waterspouts: all thy waves and thy billows are gone over me. Yet the LORD will command his loving kindness in the daytime, and in the night his song shall be with me, and my prayer unto the God of my life."* We must magnify the goodness and love of God once more. The reason we sink in despair is because, like Peter, we are focusing on the rage of the storm more than love of the Savior. If your hope is in Christ, then you are on solid ground. Oftentimes it is in our "weak" days that His strength is revealed. If it takes the waves crashing upon me and the thunder rolling, for me to see that He has the power to make me walk on water and endure the storm, then so be it! Trust Him and rejoice in the fact that His love will never fade!

FOR TODAY
Read

Psalms 42 (Morning)
What strengthened the joy of the Psalmist (vs. 4)?

2 Corinthians 1:1-7 (Noon)
Through the comfort God gives us, what are we called to do?

Psalms 55 (Night)
According to verses 12-13, why was David in such heartache?

Romans 8:28 reminds me that what I might think are blunders can undoubtedly be His wonders

Day 28

The "us four and no more" mentality should be foreign to the church. I remember in Bible College I began to develop an "elitist" attitude. It became easy for me to put God and His ways in some doctrinal box and to set myself up as a sanctified big shot. You see, the later part of 1 Corinthians 8:1 says, "...*Knowledge puffeth up, but charity edifieth.*" I was often "puffed" up over how much I "knew." I took pride in how I used spiritual jargon or could intelligently quote vast amounts of scripture. I boasted in my knowledge and keeping of religious principles, which were oftentimes just man made preferences.

Now, understand that by no means am I advocated a life of ignorance. We are called to "*Study to shew ourselves approved unto God (2 Timothy 2:15).*" We're servants of love, but we're also students of His Word. Becoming "puffed up" is when God's Word is a textbook of rules and regulations to us and not a living book that flows forth love, hope, and grace. When it simply fills our minds, but does not grip our hearts. It begins the moment that I no longer read God's Word with humbleness and a passion to lovingly edify others, but with a pious stubbornness and a desire to merely justify my preferences.

The study of theology is to be mixed with the humility of the heart and the wonder of the soul. To have a child-like awe and a servant-hood aspiration. The essence of holiness is availability not intelligibility. It's not when I can package my Christianity, crossing all the "t's" and dotting every "i", but when I just cherish Jesus and long for others to come to that point as well. Don't be an elitist. Don't be the "snob" conformed in the crowd, be the servant transformed by His love. One day Jesus will return and judge the "elite", and believe me when that day comes, no one will want to be part of a clique. Isaiah 2:10-11 states, *"Enter into the rock, and hide thee in the dust, for fear of the LORD, and for the glory of his majesty. The lofty looks of man shall be humbled, and the haughtiness of men shall be bowed down, and the LORD alone shall be exalted in that day."*

FOR TODAY
Read

Galatians 2 (Morning)
What wrongdoing did Peter commit causing Paul to admonish him?

Isaiah 66:1-2 (Noon)
As stated in verse 2, what are two heartfelt actions that God desires?

James 2 (Night)
Think about verses 1-5. Are favoritism, partiality, & "cliques" found in Christianity today? Can you think of an example?

He is All in All

He is all we need,

for daily victory.

Only on our knees

with a simple plea

We ask for grace

Strength to fight for today

But our battles He will face

Thus, we give Him the praise***

Day 29

In Matthew 13, Jesus speaks a parable about a farmer who sows seed on four different types of soils. In the same passage He tells His disciples that the truth of the parable is about how people respond to the Word of God. The first response regards those who hear but don't understand it, so satan deceives them into thinking they don't need it. For some, it is the fact that they want "more" proof. They want God to yield to their terms, if their going to believe. For others, they allow their friends to make their decisions for them. I remember one time witnessing to a teenager and I could tell that he was very attentive to what I was saying, that is, until his buddy came by. When his friend heard me, he just started smirking as if wanting to say, "This is bogus man! Don't believe it." After that, the teen I was witnessing to changed his mood completely and began to disregard anything that was said. How sad.

The second response Jesus speaks of, are those who hear and gladly receive God's Word, but after several hardships, they quit. They think that Jesus is going to simply bless them materially and make their lives a lot smoother, not realizing that great blessings can come even in trials, because God is the God of all comfort and He seeks to strengthen us through the tough times. It's as if they are just "trying on Jesus". They are almost like a fair weather fan. Please understand that salvation is not "flippantly trying on Jesus", it is FULLY TRUSTING IN JESUS.

The third reaction in hearing the gospel is that those who hear and receive will still not let go of their love for the world. They are distracted, preoccupied with climbing what they consider the ladder of success. Instead of growing in Christ as a believer, they get tangled in striving for that better job position. They get "wrapped up" spending most, if not all of their free time looking for ways to be entertained, rather than seeking to be edified in the faith and honoring God with their lives. Sadly, by and large, the American church has settled for this. It is a convenient Christianity, but nothing more. No real power. No lasting fruit. *1 John 2:15-17 states, "Love not the world, neither the things that are in the world. If any man love the world, the love of the Father is not in him. For all that is in the world, the lust of the flesh, and the lust of the eyes, and the pride of life, is not of the Father, but is of the world. And the world passeth away, and the lust thereof: but he that doeth the will of God abideth for ever."*

Finally, the last response to the gospel is those who not only hear it, but also understand, receive, and LIVE it. Understanding is what sets them apart from the reaction of those mentioned first in Christ's parable. They not only acknowledge their overwhelming need for Jesus as Savior and Lord, but also they realize that there is much more to life than what is on the surface. They live with an eternal perspective, striving to grow and glorify God. I hope we all understand that as we surrender to God's purposes, we will experience satisfaction in His presence. I simply ask you, what kind of response have you given towards the gospel of Jesus?

FOR TODAY
Read

Matthew 13 (Morning)
In verses 53-58, what was the response of the people in Jesus' home town and why did He not do many miracles?

Luke 8:1-18 (Noon)

John 12 (Night)
Why wouldn't the chief rulers confess Christ?

The Christian life is not a "try harder" religion, but it is a TRUST HIM RELATIONSHIP

Day 30

Paul wrote in Romans 8:6, *"For to be carnally minded is death; but to be spiritually minded is life and peace."* There have been many times in my life that when someone asked me what I was doing, I would reply to the effect of "Nothing much, just thinking." Of course, almost always they would say with great sarcasm, "Oh, well that could be dangerous for you." It is a simple joke and yet it holds some truth. You see, every spiritual struggle starts with a person's thought life.

We must realize that the fruit of wickedness can only come when one allows a "sinful seeded" thought to take root in his mind and grow. Proverbs 23:7 states, *"For as he thinketh in his heart, so is he."* This is why Jesus revealed that if a man looks with lust upon a woman, he has already committed adultery through a perverse mind. So, how do we combat impure thoughts?

Perhaps we just don't use our brains at all. We amuse and entertain ourselves until we die. After all, amuse means to "not think." This is obviously a wrong assessment. Every Christian is commanded to be a thinker. We are called to grow in the knowledge of Christ (2 Peter 3:18) and faithfully study God's truths (2 Timothy 2:15). Undoubtedly, a life of victory will always begin with a mind of purity.

Notice what Paul urged the believers in Philippi to do, *"Finally, brethren, whatsoever things are true, whatsoever things are honest, whatsoever things are just, whatsoever things are pure, whatsoever things are lovely, whatsoever things are of good report; if there be any virtue, and if there be any praise, think on these things (Philippians 4:8)."* The prophet Isaiah declared, *"Thou wilt keep him in perfect peace, whose mind is stayed on thee: because he trusteth in thee (Isaiah 26:3)."*

To combat wicked thoughts we must consistently pray to and think upon God Himself. Think upon His goodness, His grace, and His love. Think upon His promises and the blessings He has given you. Ultimately, fill your mind with His Word. Hebrews 4:12 affirms, *"For the word of God is quick, and powerful, and sharper than any twoedged sword, piercing even to the dividing asunder of soul and spirit, and of the joints and marrow, and is a discerner of the thoughts and intents of the heart."* His word cuts deep, but it does so to uproot our wicked imagination and replace it with God's truths and revelation. A holy mind: this is where life and peace abounds.

FOR TODAY
Read

2 Corinthians 10 (Morning)
Verse 12 reveals a pervasive problem that is found in the mindsets of many Christians. What is it describing?

Psalms 119:97-104 (Noon)
How did David gain understanding and insight?

Psalms 40:5 & Matthew 6:24-34 (Night)
Have you ever just thought about the great fact that God thinks about you?

Salvation's Sunshine

As the rays of the sun, or a stars effervescence
Bursting forth with glory
So you banished the chilling darkness
Imparting life and victory
Sunlight fills each day
Gone are the empty endeavors
Warm presence envelops the way
*May Your Glory shine forth forever****

Day 31

Acts 9:29 says, *"And he (Paul) spake boldly in the name of the Lord Jesus, and disputed against the Grecians: but they went about to slay him."* What a fervor and devotion Paul had regarding the spread of the gospel! Throughout his life, dangerous as it would be, Paul confidently and consistently preached salvation through Jesus Christ. Sadly, such boldness today is a rarity amongst professed believers.

Many, including myself, do not truly know what it is like to "risk it all" simply by declaring God's truth. In America, criticism towards Christianity is growing, but true hostility is scarce. Of course, there are many other countries where persecution abounds. Often I wonder whether I would preach just as strongly as I do today, if I were one day faced with suffering on account of the gospel message. Would I be faithful? Would you?

Notice what Hebrews 4:14-16 states, *"Seeing then that we have a great high priest, that is passed into the heavens, Jesus the Son of God, let us hold fast our profession. For we have not an high priest which cannot be touched with the feeling of our infirmities; but was in all points tempted like as we are, yet without sin. Let us therefore come boldly unto the throne of grace, that we may obtain mercy, and find grace to help in time of need."* The amazing reason why Paul could boldly preach is because he boldly prayed. He knew that Jesus experienced all our pains and agonies, and in the midst of it all, He overcame sin and the world. He knew that he would most assuredly *"find grace to help in time of need."*

Perhaps the reason fear can easily overcome our hearts and stop our mouths from sharing the message of Christ is that we do not *"come boldly to the throne of grace."* Some believers do not understand the sufficiency and power of God's grace nor have their hearts been convinced that there is a lavish supply for daily victory. Paul said, *"I know whom I have believed, and am persuaded that He is able... (2 Timothy 1:12)"* Is this your heart's song and mind's assurance? Has your prayers for help and guidance been just rehashed rhetoric with no deep trust that God will sustain and strengthen you? Trust and rejoice in the fact that God through *"...his divine power has given unto us all things that pertain unto life and godliness, through the knowledge of him that hath called us to glory and virtue* (2 Peter 1:3)."

FOR TODAY
Read

2 Timothy 1 (Morning)
What kind of "spirit" has God given us (vs. 7)?

Colossians 4:1-5
What did Paul request of his fellow believers?

Acts 1 (Night)
After the ascension of Christ, and just before Pentecost, what did the believers continue to do?

Far too many people today are 'Christianized' but not 'Crucified.' They are dead with principles instead of alive with power!

67

Day 32

Often when a church has services that last half or even a whole a week, the meetings are called "revival." Most realize that this only emphasizes the need for a "spiritual awakening"; however, for a believer to be "revived," means that at some point in his Christian walk he "died." Paul wrote to the Christians at Ephesus, *"And you hath he quickened (*made alive*), who were dead in trespasses and sins* (Ephesians 2:1)." When you got saved, not only were your sins forgiven, but also you came alive spiritually. You were made a new person. There shouldn't be any "talk" of dying spiritually again.

Nowhere in scripture do we read of frequent meetings being held where people met for the purpose of being "revived." We do however read about lives being changed by the power of God and the presence of God showing up in mighty ways in the hearts and lives of believers. But in these acts of holy fire and sweet surrender, it is evident that each believer is indeed never the same and remains a humble vessel for the Master's use. They do not get back in a "rut" within six months. No, they grow and flourish, which is something that the Church of today knows little of. I believe we Modern Christians are the only people who are somehow willing to let everyone know that we have been "dormant" for Christ for weeks. By this I mean that we hand out flyers and announce in advance that we are having a meeting that will revive us in spiritual focus, boldness, and a desire for purity. Yet, as a child of God, such "reviving" should already be laid claim to in our lives.

So, we must be careful not to have the view that one preacher did when he said, "Revival is like a bath. It will get you clean, but you'll need another one sooner or later." Richard Wurmbrand, founder of Voice in the Martyrs, once stated, "W*hen I came to America, I heard for the first time in my life the term "revival." We don't have this notion of revival in my country. I have* *been born 72 years ago. I have never been revived, I just live...I have been "born again" 45 years. I have never felt a need of revival, I just live."* The lost need to be "revived" and made alive in Christ, but what many Christians need is to have a heart revelation of their NEW LIFE IN CHRIST!

To me, the word "restoration" carries a better meaning as to what the church needs. Webster defines it as, "...Renewal of health and soundness...Recovery from a lapse or any bad state." There are some believers today who have fallen in the trenches of sin. Instead of being a faithful soldier for Christ, they are weak in the faith. There are some who have been wounded by trials or even by another brother or sister in Christ. They need restoration. You may think, "Big deal. What does it matter about the name?" Yet, words are powerful and when it comes to spiritual renewal, we shouldn't just toss around titles for church gatherings without realizing what they imply. I hope we all learn to pray, as David did, *"**Restore** unto me the joy of thy salvation... (Psalms 51:12a)"*

FOR TODAY

Read

Galatians 6 (Morning)
Annually a church may host a special evening service for an entire week, yet what should the church be willing to do every day (vs. 1—2, 10)?

Psalms 85 (Noon)
What is the pervasive theme in this passage (vs. 2, 7, & 9)?

Psalms 51 (Night)

What does verses twelve and thirteen reveal as to why some
Christians do not speak about Christ?

_____

***God is just as mighty in our valley of distress as He is on our
mountain top of success***

Day 33

My brother is only 17 months older than me. So, you can imagine how growing up for us was a constant competition of deciding who was stronger, more athletic, taller, and so on. The truth is that I had always looked up to my brother and would often compare myself to him, especially when it came to creativity and intellect. There was just one problem: statistically, he was smarter than 98% of kids his age.

Now I was never good at math, but I knew that the task of measuring up to his knowledge was impossible. Because of this, I would easily get discouraged and end up studying very little in school. I remember years later, when I confessed to my brother at how I envied his intellect; he told that for a long time he envied my ability to make friends and my treasured humor.

Paul wrote to the believers in Corinth, "*If the whole body were an eye, where were the hearing? If the whole were hearing, where were the smelling? But now hath God set the members every one of them in the body, as it hath pleased him* (1 Corinthians 12:17-18)." He was reminding them that were not to try to compare themselves with one another, but to realize the different "abilities" that God had given each one of them. We cannot all be pastors (There would be no more fried chicken left in the world). We cannot all be Sunday school teachers, worship leaders, or great singers. However, all of us have unique personalities, various gifts, and different trades. Each one can be used for the supreme purpose of magnifying God.

David declared in Psalms 34:3, "*O magnify the LORD with me, and let us exalt his name together.*" This calling is extended to every believer in Christ. For some, God has chosen them to uplift Him by their singing, for others, by their carpentry. Simply, where you are at, be available to His leading. Always be ready to magnify Him. Don't be disheartened over what others can do and what you cannot do, but delight yourself in the wonderful truth that God can use and shine through any willing heart.

_____

FOR TODAY
Read

1 Corinthians 12 (Morning)
What would happen today if the church would live out verses twenty five & twenty six?

Psalms 133 (Noon)
According to this passage, when is God's blessing given?

Romans 12 (Night)
List the statements Paul wrote regarding how we are to treat fellow believers; likewise, the statements that deal with how we are to behave toward those in the world.

_____

*** *Don't allow your tears to drown you in fear*
For they cause you to clasp tighter onto the hands of the One Who,
undoubtedly one day, will wipe them away forever ***

Day 34

Ephesians 4:29 says, *"Let no corrupt communication proceed out of your mouth, but that which is good to the use of edifying, that it may minister grace unto the hearers."* Often when I would read this verse, I thought about curse words, blasphemies, words spoken in anger etcetera. However, the word corrupt bears the meaning of "worthless words." It may seem farfetched, but you can hear "corrupt" speech from the pulpit just as easily as you can from the nearest pub. Now, before you mentally fling tomatoes at me, you must understand that in no wise am I stating that going to a worship service and going to Wal-mart will bring about the same results. No. What I am seeking for you to see is that no matter the setting and even the "way" we says things, our spiritual conversations can fall so far from true edification. Even if what we say sounds good, it can be mixed with plenty of error. Sadly, a half truth can be deadlier than a full lie. The half truth may be distorted, but it is also decorated. One statement in particular that is often used is "Fake it till you make it."

Out of every so called "edifying" phrase that I have heard, no other has given me such disgust in the pit of my stomach as this one. I suppose to some people it appears to be words of comfort. It is said for the preacher discouraged by the actions of his congregation. If he is depressed, he must simply ACT like he's not so others won't have to deal with his problems and see the wounds. It is said for the lady who has been hurt by someone and harbors a hint of resentment toward them, so rather than seeking reconciliation, all she must do is put on a plastic smile, acting as if they're best friends. The Christian life never calls for hypocrisy! If you fake it, you will never "make it." We live by FAITH, not by FAKING.

Let's imagine for a moment that you are walking down some street and you see a man get hit by a car. You quickly run to him in a panic not knowing what to do except call 911. You stand over his bleeding and bruised body trying to console him and let him know that the paramedics are on the way, but before you finish even one sentence, a man walks over to the hurt individual and attempts to pick him up on his feet. Furiously you shout, "What are you doing!?" "Oh, this guy needs to stop worrying about his condition and just act like he is ok. He will get better in time, as long as he pretends nothing happened." Wouldn't you be the first to request that this strange man be locked up in a mental hospital? Well, how dare we ever gloss over the wounds of a soul by giving some cliche' answer that is WORTHLESS.

When a person takes these words to heart and strives to "make it", he inevitably ends up worse than before, because he tried in his own efforts to muster up feelings of joy and strength. All over the country, there are scores of believer's who do this. They wear a mask to hide their hurts. They are afraid. Scared of what others might think and fearful over how long they have to "fake it till they make it." Mark it down, when someone tells you to do this, what they really mean is that they don't want to take the time to "bear" your burden and walk that extra mile with you down the path of genuine consolation. James 5:16 says, *"Confess your faults one to another, and pray one for another, that ye may be healed."* Imagine that! Believer's actually coming together and revealing their scars, not in pride or out of some duty, but for RESTORATION and a REALIZATION that NONE of us can "make it" without the Spirit of Christ living within.

Romans 12:15-16 states, *"Rejoice with them that do rejoice, and weep with them that weep. Be of the same mind one toward another. Mind not high things, but condescend to men of low estate. Be not wise in your own conceits."* When I am burdened under the weight of discouragement or just plain

74

weariness, I don't want buttered up words or a counterfeit smile, I want someone who is willing to pray with me, while shedding tears. I want someone who will remind me of God's faithfulness by their own willingness to take the time to hear the pleading of my soul, without some cynical or pious attitude. Give me love! His love! Be genuine! I do realize that God gives us discernment and we don't need to be wearing all our feelings on our sleeves. Yet, the truth is that we don't have to "fake" anything in life, even when we battle with our feelings. We must trust in the personal working of the indwelling Holy Spirit. You may not feel like forgiving one who has wronged you, but when you turn your eyes back on God, believing that through His Spirit He will give you the power to forgive, then you will be able to conquer that "root of bitterness" in your life. Have faith in God's working, be compassionate to others, and be sincere in your love.

FOR TODAY
Read

Luke 12 (Morning)
What is the "leaven of the Pharisees" (Vs. 1)?

Philemon (Noon)
What was Paul's praise toward Philemon (vs. 5)?

1 Samuel 23 (Night)
How was Jonathan instrumental in encouraging David?

Lot made a choice I'm sure for his family and future but not with his faith. Let us never be as unmindful as Lot. Do not seek the field of happiness, without first seeking God's face and holiness

Day 35

It is a verse that many people know well, yet it is also one of the most misquoted verses in the Bible. I am talking about Philippians 4:13 in which Paul writes, *"I can do all things through Christ which strengtheneth me."* It is a wonderful truth that through Jesus we have victory over sin, but some mistakenly claim this verse teaches that in Christ they can "get rich", increase their possessions, or become some big shot in the world's eyes. They use this verse as simply a buffer for the fulfillment of their own wants.

Jesus is viewed as simply the means to obtain their dreams. Yet, for Paul, his dream and desire was Jesus! You see, if you read the verses prior to verse 13, you will realize the great truth that Paul was teaching believers. Paul writes in verses 11-12, *"Not that I speak in respect of want: for I have learned, in whatsoever state I am, therewith to be content. I know both how to be abased, and I know how to abound: every where and in all things I am instructed both to be full and to be hungry, both to abound and to suffer need."*

The "I can do all things" that Paul was speaking of was not some cheap motivational talk, but a precious truth that through some of the deepest sorrows and toughest sufferings of life, we can still be content. This is a far cry from what some teach, but it is nonetheless true. Notice what Hebrews 13:5-6 states, *"Let your conversation be without covetousness; and be content with such things as ye have: for he hath said, I will never leave thee, nor forsake thee. So that we may boldly say, The Lord is my helper, and I will not fear what man shall do unto me."*

Such contentment is planted firmly in Jesus Christ. It is faith in the promise that Jesus said *"I will never leave thee nor forsake thee.*" Can you boldly say to others that God is your helper even in the midst of heartache? Why can we be "content" even in tough circumstances? Because Jesus is powerful enough to give us grace and peace to endure. Because He is powerful enough to transform my trials into triumphs not simply by delivering me from them, but by strengthening and shaping my life through them for His glory! The purpose of it all is that I might boldly declare to everyone, *"The Lord is my Helper...I will not fear!"*

FOR TODAY
Read

Philippians 4 (Morning)
What does verse six teach regarding worries?

Psalms 62 (Noon)
Mark each statement dealing with the "heart." What do they mean?

Proverbs 11 (Night)
What does this passage teach regarding riches?

On the Cross He bore our sins, so that we might conquer and be free from our sin. He Experienced Rejection that we might receive Everlasting Redemption. He Suffered Abandonment that we might be Adopted. Jesus Died Suffering Thirst that we might have 'Rivers of Living Waters' flowing through us. His Body was beaten, bloodied, and bruised that He might fashion one glorious body, His bride, the Church. He Became Despised by many that He might bring Delight to all and become the Desire of many nations. He was the Persecuted, Innocent Lamb that He might be the Perfect Intercessor of the Saints. He was Lifted up in Agony but would ultimately Ascend into Glory. On the cross, one of His first cries in utter pain was "WHY AM I FORSAKEN?" but His final cry in ultimate power was, "IT IS FINISHED!" Oh the Splendor of Calvary!

77

Day 36

At the very outset of Acts 8, a devout Christian named Philip traveled to the large city of Samaria and, *"preached Christ unto them."* (Acts 8:5) God used him to heal the sick and spiritually afflicted, and through his preaching of the gospel, many people came to know Christ. Acts 8:8 states that, *"there was great joy in that city."* Interesting enough, Philip was one of the first deacons within the New Testament Church. Far too many Christians today have yet to realize that the New Testament deacons were not only chosen to aid in the care of widows and certain families, but also they were appointed to preach the gospel! The first recorded martyr of the Christian church was Stephen who also was a deacon. His testimony of boldness in the gospel and compassion through suffering is astounding. But I digress.

My focus for now is Philip. You see, by all standards of the American church today, Philip's work in Samaria was a huge success. It would have been unthinkable for him to leave. Yet, in the midst of such a seemingly great ministry opportunity, verse 26 of Acts 8 says, *"And the angel of the Lord spake unto Philip, saying, Arise, and go toward the south unto the way that goeth down from Jerusalem unto Gaza, which is desert."* That's it? The desert? I am certain that there were many believers who sought to dissuade Philip from doing this. Perhaps they would have said, "What are you doing man? Things are going great here. People are getting saved, the church body is rapidly increasing, and who knows what lies ahead for you!" It seemed sheer nonsense to leave such a thriving ministry and journey into the desert.

Yet, a long time before Samaria, Philip realized that the call of the Christian life is about unreserved availability to wherever the Holy Spirit leads! (I will summarize what happened next, but I urge you to read Acts 8 for yourself) He immediately obeyed and traveled to the desert. I don't believe he was "wondering" what to do next, I believe he simply waited on the Spirit's guidance. As he walked in the desert, Philip saw a stunning, royal chariot. It carried the chief treasurer for the queen of Ethiopia. It was then that the Holy Spirit told him to go to that man. Philip ran. He ran with urgency and eagerness. The closer he got to the chariot, the more he could hear the Ethiopian reading from the book of Isaiah! That day another soul was added to the kingdom of God. For some Christians today, they may think, *Big deal it was just one person. Philip left a massive city for this?* Yet, church history records that the same treasurer went back to his country with the glorious gospel and reached thousands for Christ.

Be available to God's leading. Be careful not to speculate and get caught up over what seems "implausible" or "unconventional." Truly, God's ways are higher than ours. Realize that God's Spirit will never lead you from the teaching of His Word, but also realize that sometimes we do not "fully" follow God because we are simply worried about the preferences and criticisms of man. We all must come to the place where we can pray, "God take me to the desert where I simply listen to your voice and see that the Christian walk is about availability, not just activity."

FOR TODAY
Read

Acts 8 (Morning)
What is important about the Ethiopian's statement found in verse thirty one?

Acts 16:1-10 (Noon)
In these verses, what did the Holy Spirit do as Paul and Luke sought to minister in different places?

John 21(Night)

What did Jesus say to Peter when he asked about the call of John?

***The Sinner's Plea

Shackles that are heavy and real,

A life dominated by satan's terrible will;

Condemned to death then eternal pain

My hope fades by the sight of sin's stain

O' wretched man I must cry!

Nothing can save such a worm as I!

Yet, had I known of His marvelous grace

And the beauty of love in His Holy face;

Then would I have flown to His arms and been at rest!

But I can do nothing, because you never confessed.

You never spoke of His love for me

Alas! Perhaps, my state was much to pity.

However, the truth of grace's members

Is that it abounds to the chiefest of sinners.

Should not this blessed song be sung,

Through word and deed for sinners to be won?

O' please dear justified saint,

Confess Christ's grace before its too late***

Day 37

I believe only once in my life have I completed a puzzle. Sadly, as I recall, it was just a 150 piece set! Even in something so trivial, I still felt accomplished and a bit more intelligent. Quite often, when a major task is finished, whether it is business related or just a simple home "to-do" list, there is a sense of satisfaction and relief. Completion gives way to rest.

This is why Paul said in Colossians 2:10, *"And ye are complete in Him, which is the head of all principality and power."* We are "complete" in Christ. What does this truly mean? On the cross, just before Jesus died, He cried out "it is finished!" He died to bear the sins of the world. He paid the price that the Law of God demanded for every soul. It was finished and it was final.

Just as Hebrews 10:10 states, *"By the which will we are sanctified through the offering of the body of Jesus Christ once for all."* There is such an overwhelming joy and continual satisfaction to know that when I receive the love and life of Jesus into my heart, I am made FULLY WHOLE! Paul again echoes this same truth in 1 Corinthians 1:30-31, in which he writes, **"But of him are ye in Christ Jesus, who of God is made unto us wisdom, and righteousness, and sanctification, and redemption: That, according as it is written, He that glorieth, let him glory in the Lord."**

Because of redemption, we can rest in and enjoy the grace of God. How sad it is that there are Christians who still believe they need some kind of a "second work" from God to live victoriously. Some even think that although Jesus saved them, they have to struggle to "live for" God in their own power and strength. Rejoice my friend, for you are COMPLETE in Jesus! He is enough for today, tomorrow, and forever! True holiness is manifested when we stop focusing on our self righteous efforts and start resting in the finished work of Jesus Christ.

It is when we stop fighting and start trusting that the indwelling work of the Holy Spirit becomes all the more tangible within our hearts and uplifting to our minds. I leave you with a wonderful promise stated in 1 Thessalonians 5:23-24, *"And the very God of peace sanctify you **wholly**; and I pray God your **whole** spirit and soul and body be preserved blameless unto the coming of our Lord Jesus Christ. **Faithful** is he that calleth you, who also will **do it**."* (Emphasis added)

FOR TODAY
Read

Colossians 2 (Morning)
How could the strict teaching that Paul wrote about in verses 20-23 be applied today?

John 17:1-10 (Noon)
What is "life eternal"?

Hebrews 10 (Night)
In verses 22-23, what did the writer of Hebrews urge the believers to do?

Psalms 133:1 states, "A Song of degrees of David. Behold, how good and how pleasant it is for brethren to dwell together in unity!" If unity and love is the language of heaven, then strife and bitterness is the language of hell

Day 38

Several years ago, my oldest son, who was only about two at the time, gave my wife two small flowers that he found outside. He called out to her and said, "Here's mommy!" Her heart melted. My mind wandered. I looked at her overjoyed reaction, and then at her small, wilted prize and thought *how amazing it is that as parents no matter how small, tainted, and ordinary a gift from your child is, you would not trade it nor the bright and heartfelt look in their eyes for anything.* As I pondered on this, my heart became overjoyed.

In part, it was because I was enjoying the moment in time, but more so because God was speaking to me through my son's meek act. *"How much more"* were the words that kept flowing through my mind. Jesus said in Luke 12:28 *"If then God so clothe the grass, which is to day in the field, and to morrow is cast into the oven;* **how much more** *will he clothe you, O ye of little faith?"* Often when declaring God's care for His children, Jesus would use the words *"how much more."* God began to say to me, "Josh, how much more. How much more do I love and delight in the praises and humble offerings of my children? How much more do I joy over the soul that comes with a simple, seeking heart to please me?"

Immediately, I thought about how often I would try to "bring a gift" to God, the times that I would strive to serve Him and yet my mind would constantly be filled with distressing thoughts such as *I am inadequate. It's not enough. God wants my best and I'm not cutting it.* So many times I have heard preachers say, "God wants your best and then He'll do the rest and be pleased." Yet, how are you to know what your best is and when you actually do it? Truly, this can easily turn into a tug o' war of emotions and doubt. Every step taken turns into a question of whether you "gave it your all." It is like the army slogan, "Be all that you can be." It sounds noble and grand to implement such thinking into the Christian life, but it is so far from true, sanctified living. All that **I** can be is nothing. It is only when my "all that I can be" shifts into "Christ is all in me" that I please and honor God. Sadly, this "do it your best" attitude, if not properly examined, will become something tangible like a list of rules, standards, and regulations.

Somehow, in order to give your best, you must "check off" every principle and preference you have upheld. Wearing a tie? Check. Listening to only hymns? Check. I had, for a time, bought into such a lie that God was not pleased unless I had heeded to every single fundamental preference and conservative principle under the sun. It was as if simply having a heart and hunger for Christ was not enough. It was weak and wilted and what I needed was a "finer, fancier" faith where I prayed like a King James translator and looked like the CEO for a suit company. I thought it was only then that my gifts to God could be pleasant in His sight.

I can't imagine my wife ever berating my son over the flowers he gave her simply because they were not from a florist, they were not enough, or they were too small and dirty. Regrettably, this is often our view of God with our *fundamental* way of thinking. In reality, so many *standards* we deem as priceless treasures are probably to God just about as desirable as tailpipe smoke in the face, because we do so much in pride and self righteous ambition rather than simple, humble adoration.

True Christianity is not found in the adornment of standards, but in AVAILABILITY TO THE SPIRIT. Psalms 103:14 states, *"For he knoweth our frame; he remembereth that we are dust."* Understand that we are only the dust of the ground. We are the soil. That is it. Christ is the seed, He is the water, and He is the sun. If we want life and fruit, if we want to be pleasing, we are only to be available to the planting and power of Jesus. Look no further than the distraught man who came to Christ, desiring that He heal his son. His cry to Jesus was, *"Lord, I believe; help thou mine unbelief!* (Mark 9:24)" He knew that no matter how much faith he could "muster" in his own abilities it was still *flawed faith* unless rooted in the grace of Christ.

When I saw Ethan giving Stephanie those two tiny flowers, I saw myself yielding up my wilted life, my flawed faith and saying "Here's Lord! Help Thou me to glorify You through Your Son!" And for a moment, with the eyes of my heart, I could see God smiling. Don't get caught up in the stress and strain of legalism, just rejoice in the glorious wonder that God rejoices over you as His dear child.

FOR TODAY
Read

Zephaniah 3 (Morning)
What kind of reaction is magnified of the Lord regarding the salvation of His people?

Jeremiah 29:1-13 (Noon)
What similar truth does Jeremiah 29:11, Psalms 40:5, and 1 Peter 5:7 reveal?

Isaiah 62 (Night)
Try to look up what Hephzibah means?

Never think that you must rush yourself in reading your Bible and prayer, so that you can get back into your daily, busy routine of life. Communion with God is the heartbeat of your life! Take the time to give Him thanks*

Day 39

In Luke chapter 9, Jesus said to his disciples, "*And whatsoever house ye enter into, there abide, and thence depart. And whosoever will not receive you, when ye go out of that city, shake off the very dust from your feet for a testimony against them* (vs. 4-5)." Before His crucifixion, He commissioned His disciples to go out and preach that "the kingdom of heaven is at hand." They were to go with humble hearts, fully relying on the Lord's provision and care. They would be preaching pilgrims, traveling testifiers of the kingdom of God. To find lodging was not an easy task, though hospitality was common in their day. Those who would gladly receive them were not just showing an innate kindness but also revealing that they supported the disciple's message.

Blessings would abound for those who not only received the message of the kingdom with open hearts, but also received the disciples with open homes. However, to those who would exude hatred and execute fierce tactics sending them away, the disciples were to shake off the dust of their feet and keep going. Such an action was not limited to the disciples when Jesus was on earth, but Paul and Barnabas also followed this pattern in Acts 13:50-52, "*But the Jews stirred up the devout and honourable women, and the chief men of the city, and raised persecution against Paul and Barnabas, and expelled them out of their coasts. But they shook off the dust of their feet against them, and came unto Iconium. And the disciples were filled with joy, and with the Holy Ghost.*"

For years, I wondered why Jesus commanded His disciples to do this and how one could apply such an action today. I realized that it was to be "a testimony against them (those who indignantly rejected)", but was that it? I fully believe that when Jesus told His disciples to shake the dust off their feet, He was not simply making a statement for the generation at hand. His command echoes forth for all generations of believers.

Foremost, for a disciple to shake the dust off his feet signified that he did all he could through the Spirit's leading. He preached faithfully, but not forcibly. It was a testimony against the angry, obstinate rejection of others. In our zeal to witness, we must be reminded of John's writing, *"Marvel not, my brethren, if the world hate you. We know that we have passed from death unto life, because we love the brethren. He that loveth not his brother abideth in death* (1 John 3:13-14)." Indeed, when we share the gospel, we must pray for prepared hearts and understanding minds. However, we also must realize that the "god of this world" has blinded many minds and hardened many hearts towards the light of the gospel. We are called to plant and water, but praise God that He gives the increase!

Finally, when a disciple would shake the dust off his feet, it was not just an outward removal of dust, but also an inward removal of hindrances. It was a signification of tossing aside bitterness. He would not allow the disdaining attitudes from that city to follow him to the next. He realized that his joy came not in good circumstances, but in Jesus Christ. How often do some strive to share the gospel in earnest, but find that they are met with more challenge from scoffers than acceptance from others? In turn, they are embittered and make no more attempts in proclaiming Christ. For other believers, discouragement sets in after a stern rejection and they find themselves questioning the very truths they were once so willing to spread.

We must realize that some will ultimately reject the gospel, but we cannot allow their attitudes and actions to become a hindrance in our lives by casting a shadow of despair or planting a seed of bitterness. We must simply shake the dust off our feet, trusting that God will give the increase in His time.

We must rejoice in that though the whole world may stand against us, God is our certain refuge and His glory alone is our chief aim. Remember the words of Jesus, *"These things I have spoken unto you, that in me ye might have peace. In the world ye shall have tribulation: but be of good cheer; I have overcome the world* (John 16:33)."

FOR TODAY
Read

Luke 9 (Morning)
What was James' and John's attitude towards those who would not receive them (Vs. 54)? What was Jesus' response?

John 15:12-22 (Noon)
Twice in these verses Jesus gave what command to the disciples?

Acts 13 (Night)
What happened to Elymas who sought to stifle one from receiving the gospel? Some will personally reject the gospel, but there are others who will vehemently seek to deter anyone from receiving the gospel.

Prayer is not about informing God, it is all about committing to Him! It is not, 'Lord, I want you to know about so and so' but, 'Lord, I know you KNOW all things so I come to lay my burdens at your feet in my own heart. I'm letting go as I rejoice in your grace and power

Day 40

In some form or another, I have heard the same statement for almost fifteen years - "I don't have to go to church!" It may not be directly stated by certain people, but they will definitely get their point across that they do not "need" church. Now, understand that I am not referring to those who hold onto an atheistic or agnostic belief. I am writing about people I have met, through the years, who have claimed to believe in God and even in, for the most part, the preservation of His Word. I found that many of them were at one time faithful members of a church, yet stopped going to services either due to a church conflict, or just sheer business on their part.

Excuses for non attendance are never dull. For some, they believe that their spiritual heritage will make up their personal lack of devotion. I have known of a family to leave a church because they were angry over the fact that the pastor did not eat a bag of tomatoes they gave him (He didn't realize they left the bag at the side door until 2 weeks later). I am not stating that there are no legitimate reasons for not going to worship services. No, often I have met people who loved God and loved church, but were completely unable to attend. Also, I fully believe that many "church going" Christians have lost sight of the call that we are to "be the" church, no just "go to" it. However, as you will find soon enough, the Bible not only teaches about the call to worship from the heart, but also about the command to worship through faithful fellowship.

If I could take 90% of all the excuses I have heard why certain professed "believers" do not go to church, it would be summarized in three main reasons. First, it would be because of PRIDE. This covers a wide range of excuses. Whether it is from the one vehemently shouting, "Church is full of a bunch of hypocrites," or from another declaring, "I don't need church, because I can worship right here in my house," their pride is the main culprit. I do sympathize with those who are disgusted by hypocrisy (Trust me; if anyone knows about hypocrites, it is the pastor!). Yet, for someone to say that they will not go back to church because of the lifestyle of Jane (or John) Doe, they are allowing others to dictate their walk with the Lord. Not to mention that, if they were honest, they would concede to the fact that they too are hypocritical in some form or another. The glaring truth is that the only good in us is JESUS CHRIST! Ephesians 4:2-3 states, *"Be humble and gentle in every way. Be patient with each other and lovingly accept each other. Through the peace that ties you together, do your best to maintain the unity that the Spirit gives* (God's Word Translation)." Often I wonder how in the world it helps the congregation or the individual, when they leave the church simply because a certain few are fakes. The answer: IT DOESN'T.

Again, the pride factor is found in one who confidently declares, "I can worship right here at home!" This sort of "loner" mentality is never good. Ecclesiastes 4:9-10 says, *"Two are better than one; because they have a good reward for their labour. For if they fall, the one will lift up his fellow: but woe to him that is alone when he falleth; for he hath not another to help him up."* The writer of Ecclesiastes seemed to have everything going for him (Most scholars, if not all, believe that it was King Solomon). He had lots of money, land, servants, and did I mention money? In the end, he realized that everything in this world is "vanity" and it is only in true companionship and ultimately honoring God that we find the greatest satisfaction. It is stated in the Talmud, "A man without companions is like the left hand without the right." Far too often, people picture themselves and their Christian walk as if they are a farmer alone in a corn field, not realizing that we are all fellow soldiers on a battlefield! Christians NEED each other.

90

We are called to edify and strengthen one another, but how can this happen if we do not FELLOWSHIP? I have had my share of heartaches both within and without the church, but I praise God that during the hardest times of my life, I met with fellow ministers once a week to simply pray and help one another! You will find that to have someone help "bear" your burdens is truly priceless. Hebrews 10:24-25 affirms, *"We must also consider how to encourage each other to show love and to do good things. We should not stop gathering together with other believers, as some of you are doing. Instead, we must continue to encourage each other even more as we see the day of the Lord coming* (GWT)."

The second factor is one that is probably the most genuine, which is pain. Yes, the reason why some do not go to church is because they have been hurt or they themselves have hurt someone in the congregation. I am not meaning in a physical sense, but more so emotionally and spiritually. For example, someone that used to be committed to worship services and invested much time in church functions, yet in the end, they wind up having their enthusiasm to serve snuffed out because they were let down by a leader in the church. This can happen if a preacher or a longstanding deacon is caught in immorality. Entire congregations implode, because so many put their trust in man's personality rather than God's truth. Proverbs 18:19a says, *"A brother offended is harder to be won than a strong city..."* Whatever the situation, when a fellow believer has been emotionally & spiritually wounded by another, sometimes in discouragement he will leave the church. When this happens, pastors have often found it easier to try to jump to the moon than to get those who have been offended and hurt back in church.

However, this problem of pain makes its way not just to those who have been slighted, but also to those who have deeply "failed" others. There are many who get out of church altogether, because they cannot forgive themselves. The memories seem to painfully linger of how they were once so faithful, and yet in a time of temptation and weakness, their integrity and reputation came crashing down. In all honesty, if ever there was a "reason" I would stay away from fellowshipping with other believers, it would be because I let many people down. To be offended is one thing, but to be the offender is a whole new matter entirely. Guilt and anxiety settles in the heart, and the fear of facing those you have wronged seems to increase. After all, even Paul found it hard to forgive John Mark when he messed up (Acts 15)! Why would anyone forgive me or you, when we fail?

Sadly, I have seen the way some so- called Christians treat believers who have committed immorality or have been battling addictions. They are not kind and are certainly not Christ-like. The reality is that we will all be judged for not only what we do, but how we respond to those who have sinned! We must realize that without the GRACE and LOVE of God we are all worthless failures! Paul declared in Romans 5:8, *"But God commendeth his love toward us, in that, while we were yet sinners, Christ died for us."* 1 John 3:1a states, *"Behold, what manner of love the Father hath bestowed upon us, that we should be called the sons of God..."* God manifested His love to us while we were sinners and by His love He has adopted those who trust Him into His family!

Have you been wronged, or have you failed someone lately? Meditate and rejoice in the love of God! Realize that we are called to forgive one another, just as Christ has forgiven us, and though many times we falter God's mercy is *"...new every morning* (Lamentations 3:23a)." Keep your eyes on Christ. Don't allow someone else to dictate your faithfulness to God and your association with fellow believers. Don't allow pain and guilt to stifle your devotion to the church. In the race of life we are called to simply keep, *"...focus on Jesus, the source and goal of our faith. He saw the joy ahead of him, so he endured death on the cross and ignored the disgrace it brought him.*

Then he received the highest position in heaven, the one next to the throne of God. ³ Think about Jesus, who endured opposition from sinners, so that you don't become tired and give up. (Hebrews 12:2-3 – God's Word Translation)."

The last factor as to why many people do not go to church is simply because of peer-pressure. Now there may be some readers thinking at this point, "Wait a minute, I'm not in elementary school anymore!" We must understand that intimidation is no respecter of persons. I remember, years ago, witnessing to a guy in college who seemed not only interested in coming to church, but also eager to learn more about Christ. However, his attention and enthusiasm almost immediately diminished when his college buddy pulled up in a large truck. As this so-called friend of his walked towards the porch where I stood, he realized that I was a "fanatic" preacher and began smugly mocking church goers. The guy I was talking with earlier changed his tune and quickly tried to find any excuse possible as to why he couldn't go to church.

John 12:42-43 states, *"Nevertheless among the chief rulers also many believed on Him; but because of the Pharisees they did not confess him, lest they should be put out of the synagogue: For they loved the praise of men more than the praise of God."* The men in this passage that believed in Jesus Christ were members of the Sanhedrin. They were wealthy and influential, yet they were too cowardly to confess that they believed Jesus was the Messiah! In Greek, "they did not confess" implies a continual action which can be interpreted, "they kept on not confessing." This literally means they continued to make excuses as to why they rejected Christ. Jesus said in Matthew 10:32-33, *"Whosoever therefore shall confess me before men, him will I confess also before my Father which is in heaven. But whosoever shall deny me before men, him will I also deny before my Father which is in heaven."* I have met a lot of "tough" people that declare, "I am not going to church, cause ain't nobody gonna run my life!" But the sad irony is that their associations were already "running" and ruining their lives. It all boils down to one question: Do you love the praise of men, more than the praise of God?

Finally, there are some people who will not go to church because they are "pressured" by those within the church. What do I mean by this? Let me illustrate. When I was a teenager, I rode the bus to church. Being homeschooled, church was normally my outlet of a social life. One Sunday in particular I remember my mom made lasagna for lunch of which I ate huge portions. When I got to church that evening, my stomach felt….awful. I usually sat towards the front of the church, so during the service I ended up having to get out of my pew and run towards the restrooms in the back. Of course, I was too late. I "tossed" almost everything I had eaten onto the carpet in front of the whole congregation.

It would be weeks before I went back to church. What little reputation I had was ruined. Do you know what happened when I eventually went back? Nothing, life went on and I ended up a year later answering the call to preach. Look, don't let fear of "judgmental glances" or pressure over "keeping up appearances" keep you from worshiping God with like minded Christians! A Christian is a follower of Christ. This is our call! Jesus is calling to us just as He Jesus declared to Peter, "...*what is that to thee? Follow thou me!"* (John 21:22)

FOR TODAY
Read

Mark 13 (Morning)
What was Christ's response to the disciples marveling over the temple?

1 Peter 2:1-11 (Noon)
List the depiction of believers as stated in verse nine? Also, concerning this world, what is a Christian described as (vs. 11)?

Ephesians 4 (Night)
What does Paul reveal concerning God's purpose for the church?

God strengthens us, when we are settled and satisfied in Him

TO THE PASTOR

You are a leader and a student. You are a soldier and a servant. You have been called to the great task of "feeding the flock," yet you must be careful not to fall into the guise of ministering out of some ritualistic duty. In our endeavors, God's grace is to be the foundation and His Love the motivation. I have had to remind myself of this often by writing certain truths that I learned throughout each year. Some are short statements, others much longer. Simply, I pray that in some way they will *"stir up the gift of God, which is in thee* (2 Timothy 1:6)."

You can copy a preacher's sermon, but you can never recreate a message from the Lord

You must be rich in His Word, before you can reach the world

Preach in jest and you will get laughs, but no love for the truth. Preach in intellect and you will get hard brains, but no soft hearts. Preach in God's power and with passion and you will get unction and action for God's glory

To live for Christ is to supremely love Christ & by faith acknowledge His working in you

Don't allow your ministerial busyness to blind you of God's matchless blessings

When you preach, they don't need a quaint conversation; they need your heart

Undoubtedly a life with a conscience clear and a pure heart produces immense Peace and procures imperative Power

Passion does not justify the exclusion of preparedness. Prepare with Passion

We sing, many times, Sweet Hour of Prayer but I believe that for some to be true to what they say it should be called Sour Minute of Prayer

The believer must find the place where Discipline and Delight, Temperance and Trust meet. Where his continuous Labor is consumed by Love and his Love is conditioned upon Truth

In the Greek, Martyr means witness and Witness means to testify or to be a present witness. The difference is when someone witnesses for Christ while living, they are to faithfully do this or they will no longer bear the mark. Yet, when someone is tried and martyred for Christ, then they will become a witness forever. By the extinguishing of their body a fire is set ablaze across the inscapes of people's hearts, which will echo and shine for all eternity. Truly, "Precious in the sight of the LORD is the death of his saints (Psalm 116:15)

Your ministerial duties, if done in the wrong mindset and motivation, can turn into drudgery rather than delight

In your preaching, do you study for content? Do you prepare for good communication? Do you live in godly conduct?

Rest in Him when the road becomes dim

Many churches during Easter and Christmas-time get so caught up on Bigger and Better Programs that they forfeit the simple power in Preaching the gospel and uplifting the Person of Jesus Christ. Many times we get so fixed on celebrating a certain "season" that we bypass Christ the Savior altogether

---

There is nothing more joyous then seeing a baby laugh and smile in your arms. Now, imagine being there as Simeon, an old faithful man to the Lord, saw wonderful baby Jesus for the first *time. Simeon's joy overflowed into song and praise. Imagine holding in your arms the One who holds the universe in His hands! Oh, what excitement and joy! But Christian know that you do hold Him, even today. You hold Him in your heart everyday! What words of celebration and praise have you spoken and sung? What message of love have you proclaimed to others? What? Come now, you have "rivers of living waters" flowing out of your life, yet you tell me it has been years since you have testified and rejoiced in Him? No fellowship at His feet hearing His Words of love and truth? No, no, believer He may be in your heart, but He's not on its throne. Come back to simple wonder. Pray for that awe and inspiration of rejoicing in Him*

***It is frightening to think that the majority of preachers that I have known spend much of their messages propagating fear more than love. They preach on how every Christian is so susceptible from falling and that if a person's devotion is only one ounce less than it was 5 minutes ago, he is backsliding. They shout how you can go so far as to be useless to God. So many sermons embrace the teaching that the Old man of the flesh battles the New man in Christ and we must feed one more than the other to win. They tell weary saints that they better be busy for Christ, for soon He will be back to judge all. They live for the 'You shouldn't and you better' speech, but where is the 'It's not you anymore, but now the Spirit of Christ' message? Where is the Spirit that is living within to build you in the image of Christ? Where is the NEW creation? Did not the Old man die, seeing that we are new in Christ? Why is it that we still have to battle, still have to fight for our precious lives, or else be doomed to failure? This is not the true gospel.

The gospel is the good news that God will not only save a poor sinner, but make him a new person in Christ, undoubtedly a holy saint. The greatest preaching is not 'Do or face wrath,' but 'it is finished now face the Love of God.' We are given a new nature where the old man is perished, not just dormant. IT IS DEAD. Just as sure as Christ has risen from the grave and is in heaven, even so His Spirit has risen in our hearts and is living in us. We have victory, not because we do something out of fear, but because we CLAIM in love that it has been done and we REST in His power alone which is mightily working in our lives. It is not some dog on dog battle of good and evil in us.

This kind of talk uplifts the influence of satan and downgrades the power of Christ. Christ's purpose in dying was to 'destroy the works of satan,' not diminish, but destroy. The irony is that so many preachers desire the congregation to live holy, thus they scream over DON'TS and shout out all the DO's without ever first establishing the very fact that it has been DONE. Living Holy is simply acknowledging the Holy One in us, which we are set apart unto Him, and daily reckoning our new nature in Christ. Sadly, we have so many weak, anemic, self righteous, pomp believers, because the one's who are supposed to be feeding the flock with Grace and Love in their hearts are actually hammering the sheep on their heads with fear and formality***